# YOU DON'T OWN ME

# YOU DON'T OWN ME

## The Life
## and Times of
## LESLEY GORE

TREVOR TOLLIVER

**Backbeat Books**

An Imprint of Hal Leonard Corporation

Published in 2015 by Backbeat Books
An Imprint of Hal Leonard Corporation
7777 West Bluemound Road
Milwaukee, WI 53213

Trade Book Division Editorial Offices
33 Plymouth St., Montclair, NJ 07042

Printed in the United States of America

Book design by Lynn Bergesen

Library of Congress Cataloging-in-Publication Data is available upon request.

ISBN 978-1-4950-2441-2

www.backbeatbooks.com

For Mom and Dad,
for never turning down the radio

# Contents

## Part One

## BABY PINK LIPSTICK AND MOTORCYCLE JACKETS

## Part Two

## SOMEPLACE ELSE NOW

Part Three

# EVER SINCE

Foreword

# A GUSHING FANBOY

I am thirty-five years old, and I have been a Lesley Gore fan my entire life. "It's My Party" was the first song I had ever committed to memory. When I was five, I used to arrange my stuffed animals into a rock band, assigning each of them a different toy instrument to jam with. I had a rabbit puppet that I would accessorize with paper-clip earrings, designating it the "girl" of the group. She got her time in the spotlight when my older brother's *60's Dance Party* album spun around to "It's My Party."

As an adult I can connect every significant phase of my life to one Lesley Gore song or another and, as I matured, there came a respect and admiration for each strand of the artist's career and life, and an enjoyment of the wide and varying styles she embraced as trends changed.

I was thrilled to have met Lesley Gore in person in Palm Springs in September 2003 at the city's summer Rocktoberfest event. She performed at a nighttime street concert, where Fabian served as a suave and witty master of ceremonies. He introduced a cavalcade of great stars—Big Bopper Jr. (the only surviving heir to the Day the Music Died in 1959), the original Tokens, Chris Montez, Little Anthony and the Imperials, and, of course, Lesley Gore. She performed a lengthy and remarkable set, singing all of her rock hits as well as a moving and clearly personal rendition of her self-penned "Out Here On My Own" from the motion picture *Fame*. She ended her time onstage with a strong, stunningly powerful, neck-veins-bulging "You Don't Own Me," and the sixty thousand people clogging Palm Springs' main avenue and hanging over balconies and rooftop railings of surrounding buildings all rose to a screaming standing ovation.

My partner and I scuttled through the crowd to get to a small table at which she would be appearing to sign autographs. When it was my turn, my eyes were already misty (don't make fun). She shook my hand and jokingly commented on the "I ♥ Lesley" button I had pinned to my sun visor. As I slid my souvenir across the table for her to sign, I began to spew out my praises—how she was my idol, how I loved her unfairly neglected *Someplace Else Now* album, and then I whipped out my official card to the Lesley Gore Fan Club as proof of my loyalty. She took the card, processed what it was I could possibly have been showing her, then, to my surprise and horror, she jumped up and extended her arms to hug me. After the hug I gushed just once more about how much I loved her, and as I stumbled away from her, I could hear her say she loved me, too. I was touched by her warmth, her kindness, and her appreciation of an individual (and slightly nutty) fan. In short, she was everything I hoped she'd be. Suffice it to say, I cried a little bit more.

You would cry, too, if it happened to you (insert trumpet bleats here).

We would cross paths again in 2006 in Los Angeles when my partner and I saw her perform during the West Coast leg of her *Ever Since* promotional tour. We were celebrating our domestic partnership, and her concert was our honeymoon; we told her so when we met her at the end of her performance, and she hugged us both and made us promise always to be good to each other. If my two chance meetings had been all I was entitled to, I would have been thrilled with that; but during the last year of her life, we struck up a friendly correspondence that is, and will remain, one of my greatest treasures. That I was allowed to call my idol since childhood a friend goes far above and beyond any and all of my wildest expectations.

Writing her biography went from being a fun and challenging pastime to a true labor of love. Compiled from interviews, extensive contemporary secondary materials, and a reexamination of her music, this record of a life is written, of course, for the artist herself, as a tribute to her fame and success, a chronological scrapbook of her struggles, disappointments, and victories; of her failures and reinventions; and of the secret private life she had to reconcile with an engineered public image. This book is also a love letter for the ardent fans who have followed her stellar fifty-year career and find it inexcusable that her story hasn't been documented sooner than this volume—as well as for the legions of new fans who rediscover her music with every passing generation and want to know more of this pop pioneer. It is also written for the casual reader who recognized the title of her anthemic signature song and has decided to indulge in a bubblegum-flavored history lesson in great rock music.

Trevor L. Tolliver, 2015

# Acknowledgments

Constructing the mosaic tiles of a human life is no small feat. There were active times in the spotlight when Lesley Gore was much more vocal and more willing to share stories and go into greater detail of the circumstances of her life and career, and still other periods of relative shyness and extraordinary privacy. Assembling these innumerable, distinct pieces into one collection would not have been nearly as enjoyable (or doable) if not for the brilliant interviewers, journalists, and writers who came before me, whose invaluable documented conversations over the last fifty years with the friendly, and sometimes reserved singer provided many of the resources used to pave the way to fashioning together one complete story. First and foremost, I thank all of you whose work is mentioned throughout the book.

I also want to thank the people who gave their time to speak with me about this project, whose personal recollections helped fill in as many gaps as possible or who were instrumental in clarifying or debunking the various myths, stories, and anecdotes that are bound to surface in a career as long and as varied as Lesley Gore's. That list includes Morris Diamond, Cevin Soling, and the late, great Phil Ramone, as well as a spunky Gore relative who requested to remain anonymous out of respect for the family—you know who you are, and I'm grateful for your trust and for the tender memories you shared. I was also thrilled to have been able to correspond with two more of my Golden Era heroes during the writing of this book—pop idol Diane Renay and legendary singer-songwriter Neil Sedaka.

For offering support, encouragement, assistance, or simple kindness along the way, I'd like to extend my gratitude to Robert Cotto, Lisa Rogak, Debra Barsha, Mark Hampton, and Detlev Hoegen. A singular thanks must go to Jack Natoli, who has been the fearless captain of the Lesley Gore International Fan Club for several decades; his generosity is matched only by his genuine sweetness, and all of us fans owe him a great debt for keeping us so well connected to our favorite singer.

A very special and resounding thank you goes to Ronny Gore, who shared her time and lovely stories of her daughter with me during a very pleasant, immensely enjoyable telephone conversation. Mrs. Gore asked that specific dates in her life and the names of certain extended family members be protected, which was a simple request I was happy to honor. Mrs. Gore is a remarkable symbol of strength and graciousness, and it's no small wonder where Lesley inherited those very same traits.

Thank you to my agent, Andy Ross, former owner of the radical 1960s hotspot Cody's Books in Berkeley, California. Andy lived and breathed one of the best, most defining American decades, and he believed in this project and its subject the moment it came his way. Thanks, Andy, for having faith in me so quickly.

Similarly, a big thanks goes to John Cerullo, Bernadette Malavarca, Wes Seeley, and the talented team at Backbeat Books for seeing the need for Lesley Gore's story and celebration of her remarkable achievements (and for responding with patience and guidance to my incessant questions). They moved quickly and efficiently to bring this to Lesley's fans.

This process wouldn't have been nearly as fun without people to help celebrate, and I'm so appreciative for the support and unconditional love of my good friends and my entire family, especially my husband, Steven Alba, and our four sons, Christian, Manuel, Rodrigo, and Jonathan—the *best* boy band of this or any other generation.

Finally, I'd like to thank Lesley Gore for her music, for her warmth, and for an all-too-fleeting friendship that was truly the treasure of a lifetime. Her music will continue to inspire. Another tremendous thank you must go to those who Lesley left behind—Lois Sasson, Michael Gore, and Ronny Gore; it could not have always been easy sharing your partner, sister, and daughter with an adoring world of strangers, but what a wonderful world Lesley made it. Thank you for letting all of us in.

# Introduction

# PUT ANOTHER DIME IN
# THE JUKEBOX

Music historians unfairly dismiss the span of time between the dual pillars of Elvis Presley and the Beatles as nothing more than a barren wasteland of mediocre songs by nice-looking but only minimally talented boys and girls, manufactured and rush released to capitalize on the expanding teenage market.

But the years from roughly 1955 to 1965 were more than some mass extinction linking the King's evolution of rock to the English Renaissance brought by the Fab Four. After all, this was the Golden Age of Rock 'n' Roll, the "simpler times" our grandparents sigh over. It was the pastel-colored *American Bandstand* period of drive-in movies, Friday night sock hops, singles on 45, Hitchcock, and giant hair. The decade symbolized '50s Americana when the boys were rebels, girls were ladies, and, still naïve of the conflict in Vietnam and of the turbulent social uprisings not yet boiled over, life was pretty good.

The music was not the tepid drivel it is so often criticized of being. Sure, the boys were fixated on their hotrods, and the girls were fixated on their boys, but the songs were fun, simple, and pure, much like the listeners who sang along with them as they cruised Main Street on Saturday nights. There was a jukebox full of new loves, unfaithful loves, and lost loves. There were myriad trends during such a brief burp of time, from the girl groups that came into vogue, led by the godmothers of pop girl groups, the Shirelles, to the emergence of folk and the California surf sound, to the introduction of Motown, to the resurrection of doo-wop, to the bizarre fad of weepy, tragic tunes of teen death and suicide that inexplicably grabbed the nation's curiosity. There was a deejay's ransom in spurious, silly dances based on physical dexterity ("The Twist," "The Locomotion"), animals ("The Monkey"), and even food ("Mashed Potato," followed by a heaping serving of "Gravy"). Cranking up the volume on AM radio was like throwing a handful of musical, colorful confetti up into the air.

The tunes may have been mild and about as controversial as a slice of apple pie, but it was far from dull. While "Johnny Get Angry" by Joanie Sommers and Bobby Vee's "Take Good Care of My Baby" didn't do much to revolutionize the industry or alter the course of rock history, they were still monster hits. Their peak positions at or near the top of the music charts are undeniable evidence of the infectiousness of the melodies, the charisma of the young stars, and the strong connection teens made to these quirky songs.

There was, to be sure, a heavy male influence within the music. After Elvis, the most dominant kids crowding the Top 10 lists were Pat Boone, Ricky Nelson, Roy Orbison, Paul Anka, Neil Sedaka, Frankie Valli, and the three Bobbys—Darin, Vee, and Vinton. Even major female acts were nurtured by masculine hands—Tina Turner's early career was dictated by evil-genius husband Ike, and million-seller girl groups like the Crystals and the Ronettes were simply instruments (albeit lovely ones) added to the dense, meshed orchestrations of uber-producer Phil Spector's "Wall of Sound."

The girls scratched and clawed for the same kind of staying power. Of course there was Connie Francis, the indisputable Queen of Pop, whose expansive recordings and flawless delivery were often too cerebral and a bit elevated from the typical teen fare, a throwback to the '50s crooners of their parents' generation. On the opposite end of the spectrum was the gravel-voiced, Cajun-peppered Brenda Lee, who racked up successful hit singles of her own; but even the spitfire Miss Dynamite herself was not impervious to a fickle buying audience. Separating these two divas was a parade of young ladies who would score big with one or two gems, then fade away into Collector's Paradise. Such was the fate of Kathy Young and her hit "A Thousand Stars"; Shelley Fabares with her lilting "Johnny Angel"; Little Peggy March's triumphant "I Will Follow Him"; wispy Connie Stevens and "Sixteen Reasons"; and Rosie and the Originals' eerie, immortal "Angel Baby."

But where were the dominant female counterparts to the Frankies and the Bobbys and the Johnnys? There would be one girl whose strong but feminine voice would lend itself to a string of enormously popular hits, placing twenty-one records on the American pop charts. Her youthful vocals would have a timbre and clarity that few other female stars of the day could match. At sweet sixteen, she would be the same age as her fans, nestling herself comfortably among them rather than toting herself above. Girls would identify with her boyfriend-induced laments, and guys would develop adolescent crushes on the pretty, fresh-faced girl gracing the covers of teen magazines. She would do what other darlings of the decade, including the indestructible Connie Francis, were unable to do: survive the British Invasion. She would later vanish, flounder, and lose her solid standing in the music scene, but still reemerge in the '70s as a thoughtful feminist singer-songwriter, and resurface yet again as a mature, energetic, introspective artist in the twenty-first century. Her remarkable career would span five decades and produce music in every one of them; her songs would receive recognition at two Grammy Award ceremonies; and her contributions to motion pictures would earn her an Oscar nomination.

Even in its totality, the illustrious career of one of teen music's founding mothers has never warranted in print anything more than a blurb in a rock encyclopedia or a few brief paragraphs online or in album liner notes that only hint at Gore's meaningful contributions and influence, suggesting a career that dried up in the late '60s with only a few highlights since, egregiously assuming a life placed on indefinite hold. This biography seeks to place her firmly into the fold of rock's early innovators, a singer who, as a solo female artist in her teens, was able to score tremendous achievements before reaching the legal adult age, which has since become standard practice in the music industry, thanks in no small part to the music, talent, and galvanizing force that first hit the radio airwaves in the spring of 1963. This biography endeavors to be, at this time at least, the most complete and accurate historical map of Lesley Gore's life and times, of the creation, evolution, and expansion of a remarkable talent. Hopefully this will not be the last time her body of work will be mined and dissected to support other valuable points of view on the bookshelf pertaining to Gore's vibrant legacy—for example, a feminist reading of her records, or an analysis through the lens of queer theory, or an evaluation of Gore and the camp imagination, or, hopefully and most importantly, the singer's own memoirs, on which she was working at the time of her sudden passing in the winter of 2015.

Light the birthday candles, turn on the phonograph, and let the party begin.

# OUT HERE ON MY OWN

By 1973—at only twenty-seven years old—Lesley Gore was already an oldie but goodie. The only job offers she was receiving were to perform with the popular nostalgia caravans touring across the country at state fairs and community playhouses where singers stomped out by the British Invasion or tossed to the wayside by the sudden and radical shifts in American rock music were given one last chance to shine before their stars flickered out cold for good. Was it really *that* long ago that "It's My Party" had thrust Lesley Gore into international fame and recognition? After a three-year blitz that saw thirteen singles in the Top 40—including smash hits like "Judy's Turn to Cry," "You Don't Own Me," "She's a Fool," and "California Nights"—had she already, years before her thirtieth birthday, become an antique that belonged to another era?

The America of 1973 was unrecognizable from the America of 1963—Vietnam, Richard Nixon, and Archie Bunker replaced tailfins, malt shops, and record hops. The squeaky clean streets of suburbia had been charred by the fires of civil unrest, and no one felt safe anymore—not after a decade that saw the political assassinations of two Kennedys and a King.

Lesley, born under the sign of the Taurus, had trouble maneuvering in this world. The Bull craves stability, is disturbed by chaos, and strives to create a secure future. Just the year before, she had released her eighth full-length album, *Someplace Else Now*, and the final product was a massive personal achievement. Free from the constraints of a paternal label that dictated the material she recorded, the record contained twelve self-penned tracks that reflected on life, love, ambition, dreams, and heartaches. Even the title of the album suggested to her fans the reemergence of a more mature artist at the peak of her creativity, a chance at a fresh career.

But no one was listening.

Following a string of unique but unsuccessful singles in the late '60s and early '70s and a series of low-paying supper club and coffeehouse appearances, the ambitious *Someplace Else Now* was supposed to return the singer to public favor, somewhere along the lines of a Joan Baez, Carole King, or Carly Simon. But fans didn't want the Lesley that ditched her bubble-coifed hair for a short-cropped, bob *au natural*; they preferred the poised, prim Lesley in a skirt and peacoat to the earth mother in bell-bottomed blue jeans. Most of all, fans—fatigued by war and exhausted by social maelstroms—wanted to escape to a simpler time, and "It's My Party" would take them there, back to the high school dances and lover's lanes. To Lesley, who desperately wanted to change her sound and craved respect as a serious songwriter, it would be a defeat to suddenly start having to look in the rearview mirror. Her past hits were of little use to her now.

Her contemporaries would find themselves locked in this same bitter syndrome. In the late '60s, Bobby Darin was driven into seclusion after being heckled mercilessly by a crowd that demanded to hear his pop classics rather than sample his new folk "message" songs. In 1971, when Ricky Nelson appeared at Madison Square Garden sporting shoulder-length hair and a honky-tonk outfit, he was booed off the stage when he refused to play his old hits in favor of a Rolling Stones cover. So devastated by the rejection, Nelson wrote and recorded the autobiographical "Garden Party," with lyrics that lamented that if memories were all he bled out, he'd "rather drive a truck."

Taureans are also notoriously withdrawn and cool, and it's usually because their most paralyzing fears, their greatest desires, and their darkest sorrows tend to run much more deeply than in other signs of the Zodiac. Living alone in an apartment on the West Coast while her family lived back East, Lesley was isolated and vulnerable. She had struck up a brief affair with a jeweler, but the fleeting companionship and whatever carapace of waning celebrity she had left could not insulate her against the failure of *Someplace Else Now*.

Reviews had been lukewarm at best, and the faint praise seemed to come from critics who had at least remembered and admired her ten years before. One claimed the album had "no real standout performances," that the vocals weren't bad, "just not as memorable. . . ." Another decided that "despite uniformly fine performances," the album was just not "attuned to the audience. . . ." And with an unintentional curtness, Barbara Lewis wrote in the Lorain, Ohio, *Journal* in 1972, "[ . . . ] It takes a super act, which Lesley is not at the moment, to fill a concert hall or huge arena."

To combat the lackluster publicity, Lesley awoke each morning, faced a clean sheet of paper on the piano, and forced herself to compose—anything to feel productive, to gather her inner reserves against her most recent failure, while looking ahead to another comeback. It was a struggle to create something decent by the end of the day—brutal, in fact—but she needed to feel like a musician, needed to sharpen the blade of her stainless steel survivor's will.

She had come too far to quit.

In 1973, without enough perspective on her old records for them to have crystallized into the pop candy corns they have since become, Lesley could not have predicted the classic status for which her records would be recognized today, a popularity of her work that would not wane in the ensuing decades. And during those lonely years in Los Angeles, she never could have imagined the remarkable triumphs still waiting ahead.

# Part One

# BABY PINK LIPSTICK AND MOTORCYCLE JACKETS

# THE SWEETIE PIE FROM TENAFLY

Just months after she arrived, Lesley Gore displayed a preternatural ear for music. Lesley Sue Goldstein was born May 2, 1946, in the great borough of Brooklyn, New York. Her father, Leo Gore—who by this time was reverting the Goldstein family surname to its Russian heritage, Gore, for a more secular sound—had been studying to become a dentist, but eventually grew wary of the daily doses of tooth decay, gum disease, and halitosis. Instead, plucky and industrious, twenty-three-year-old Leo tried his luck as an entrepreneur and, together with his brother-in-law, opened the Peter Pan Bra and Girdle Company in 1942—effectively jumping from teeth to teat.

Leo would have had plenty of inspiration to go into the ladies' garment and swimwear industry. Besides bathing and pin-up beauties being a lucrative field in the early '40s, Leo had been surrounded and influenced by solid, strong-willed women—his mother and an older sister. Another young lady, Ronny Leona, would appear early in Leo's life and take another, more significant part of his heart. Born in April 1923, Ronny was four years Leo's junior, and the pair would become childhood sweethearts, sparking a love story that would last over sixty years. "I met him when I was fourteen," Ronny told this author. "He was the boy who lived across the street." Ronny was a spirited girl, and a beauty—her broad, illuminating smile and brown, wide-set Bette Davis eyes were a perfect match for her new husband, with his gentle charm and dark, strapping Cary Grant looks. "They were really so attractive together," cooed one Gore relative.

Deciding to start a family with Leo, Ronny abandoned her career modeling hats for a fashionable Fifth Avenue boutique in Manhattan and settled into their Brooklyn apartment to prepare for their firstborn child. Ronny, probably the bravest expectant mother in all of human history, outfitted the entire nursery in white, from the drapes, to the bedding, even to the stuffed animals ardently lining the white shelves.

Almost immediately, Lesley displayed her love and fascination with sound and music. At only six months old, the baby with a tuned ear could duplicate the melody of a song. Her mother was undoubtedly amazed; her baby couldn't yet talk, but could easily learn and hum along with a melody in only an instant.

By three years old, Lesley had mastered the use of the family phonograph. Her parents, avid ballroom dancers, owned an extensive library of albums that would collapse any record collector today, including the original singles of Sarah Vaughan, Frank Sinatra, and Patti Page. Although she didn't know the names of the artists or the titles of their now-classic songs, tiny Lesley, who yet had to learn to read, knew what each record was by the color of its label. She listened to hundreds of songs and managed to memorize most of them. She wasn't above performing them, either. Visitors to the Gore home were treated to Lesley's twenty-minute sets atop the cocktail table, and as soon as her gig was over for the night, she'd toddle out of the room and into bed.

When Lesley was enrolled in kindergarten in 1950, Michael Gore was born and swiftly usurped the cherished position of baby of the family from his big sister. Leo and Ronny needed more space for their blossoming brood, so the Gores packed up and moved to Teaneck, New Jersey. Once the construction of their new dream home was completed, they moved into the nearby exclusive bedroom community of Tenafly. Tenafly in the '50s was a young family's Eden, an upper-middle-class neighborhood of block parties, summertime barbecues, and noisy games of softball in the streets that lasted well past the lampposts blinking on at sundown. Housewives reared the children and kept their homes pristine, should any of the rival social butterflies drop by to investigate and critique. Husbands crossed the bridge into New York on their daily pilgrimage to the offices uptown and kept their lawns green and cropped on the weekends. The tree-lined avenues were safe and clean, the idyllic corner of the world to bring up a little girl and boy. "It was a beautiful, beautiful place to raise children," Ronny remembered.

The four Gores settled comfortably into Tenafly routine. Every Tuesday night Ronny's friends, Ethel and Manolo, would come to the house for martinis and cha-cha dancing. Lesley's earliest memories of music around the house centered on her parents' weekly get-togethers. She and her brother would observe silently from the post at the top of the stairs, and through the banister they watched the adults mambo to Dean Martin in the living room.

Leo and Ronny were happy to instill in their children a vast appreciation of music. Their daughter was taken by early idols like June Christy, Doris Day, and Dinah Washington, the way they massaged lyrics and performed vocals rich with raw emotion; one need only listen to Washington's "What a Difference a Day Makes," which manages to sound both joyful and painfully spent, or Lena Horne's tragic and scornful "Stormy Weather," to see how the dolls of the '50s set the standards. Enamored by them, Lesley would play the records as many as fifty times until the little girl, as she explained to music writer Dawn Eden, "could lip sync literally every breath."

Leo was also quite proud of one of his own toys—a tape recorder that produced flat discs that, after dusting away the leftover acetate, became real records. Lesley fondly remembered the time her father spent standing her in front of the machine and committing her voice to a recording; she would come to acknowledge him as her first recording engineer. (In October 1953, Leo escaped the burning wreckage of a plane crash just outside Idlewild Airport. Lesley's life may have taken a completely different path had he been unable to escape.)

With the Big Apple only half an hour away from their house, Leo and Ronny wanted to ensure Lesley and Michael were exposed to the thriving, pulsating culture in the city. They were progressive parents sharing with their children what the contemporary arts had to offer. When Lesley was ten, Ronny hid her daughter beneath her mink coat and sneaked her into a midnight cabaret at Basin Street

East just so she could see Ella Fitzgerald perform live, so Lesley could hear for herself the legendary breezy, crisp voice of "Shattering Glass" Ella.

Little Michael similarly displayed a prodigal interest in music. Leo brought home an upright piano that Ronny promptly used to fill space against a wall. The boy took an immediate liking to the instrument and, perched on top of a stack of telephone books, learned to play bass chords with his left hand and tinkle out melodies with the other. Lesley was thrilled to have a collaborator, and together they crooned Eydie Gorme and Sinatra songs, as well as Gershwin show tunes. In no time at all, Michael began writing his own compositions, and the sibling duo arranged original music together. They grew from and played off of each other's talents to produce a unique songbook of their own during their after-school sessions.

To further bolster Lesley's passion for music, Leo and Ronny brought their twelve-year-old daughter to see the Broadway production of *My Fair Lady*. Lesley's eyes glowed in the footlights, awed by the grand theatrics of cockney flower girl Eliza Doolittle's rise from pauper to princess under the tutelage of phoneticist Henry Higgins (played with snide perfection by Rex Harrington on stage and in the film version). The music by Alan Jay Lerner and Frederick Loewe ranges from bawdy British camp to simply beautiful ballads, and the rags-to-riches plot made an impact on Lesley that would ultimately steer her life. She loved the musical, and when her parents asked if she'd like to see another, she enthusiastically agreed—by dragging her parents to twelve more performances of *My Fair Lady*.

Lesley knew she had a craft that needed to be practiced and honed. For starters, she eagerly signed up for summer camp talent competitions and school pageants to become accustomed to performing before a crowd.

By junior high, rock music was taking definitive form thanks to Elvis the Pelvis, and Lesley immersed herself in the developing musical style. Privately, she would pull her hair back, swivel her hips, and snarl her upper lip in front of her bedroom mirror, impersonating the swagger and slick grace of the King (later, as her own singing career took flight, she would unconsciously perform with a similar quirk—singing out of the lower right corner of her mouth). Then, in her skirt and pumps, she attended the Friday night sock hops and bopped to Connie Francis and the Everly Brothers. The hops in town were hosted by young, handsome Willy Nelson (not the same Willie of Farm Aid infamy), who was the cousin of rockabilly megastar Ricky Nelson (whose family were also Tenafly natives). Willy was the hippest promoter and party host around and was, by all accounts, "the very end." "And so dreamy, too," a close family friend gushed to this author. "He was tall, blond, and rugged. We used to go just to watch him. If all he did was stand and read from a telephone book, that would have been a very pleasant evening."

In the eighth grade, leaping onto the rock bandwagon, Lesley joined a girl group formed by her classmate, Mary Lombardi. Their repertoire consisted of only Shirelles hits, and when Lesley boldly suggested singing different material, the other girls gawked at her as if she'd just set herself on fire. The group performed at a couple of Willy Nelson rock revues, then quickly fizzled into middle-school memories.

When she turned fifteen, Lesley, in another strategic move, convinced Leo and Ronny to enroll her at the Dwight School for Girls. The Englewood private campus was renowned for its classical music program, and the high school chorus laid the paramount foundations in her musical education. She learned how to sing harmonies, how to read music, and how to sing as one element in a group. Although it was grating at first that the group performed more religious songs than she had ever heard before, she discovered she could train her voice to adapt to various genres of music, moving deftly between "The Old Rugged Cross" and "The Rock and Roll Waltz."

"I just wanted to sing, and I wanted to do it really well," Lesley said. "I'd sing something once, but it wouldn't sound the same way the second time I tried it. I was just a kid, so I was easily discouraged when I couldn't repeat something the same way again, and there was an obsession in me to try to figure out how to do it the right way every time." Unlike most young singers of her day, Lesley resolved to find a vocal coach to further train her tongue. Other teens of pop idoldom were simply thrust before a microphone without having any prior preparation. Poor Shelley Fabares was so terrified to sing that she had to record her Johnny masterpiece one chunk at a time; and Tab Hunter, who enjoyed a run of charting hits in the end of the '50s, was forced to record "Apple Blossom Time" while engineers and managers sniggered at his vocal abilities behind his back.

Upon reaching the epiphany that she needed a coach, she rushed home from school one day and gushed, "Mom, I wanna take singing lessons. That's what I wanna do."

Ronny sighed; she already had enough to do running the neighborhood carpool, tending to the tasks of the household, caring for the family—the last thing she needed was yet another chore.

Undaunted, Lesley went into the city and found Myron "Pappy" Earnhart. He saw tremendous promise in his young charge, and his pupil faithfully made the trip to his New York studio every Monday afternoon, boarding a bus on Palisades Avenue that took her across the Washington Bridge, where she would then hop on the subway downtown.

Myron Earnhart's office shared space in the mythical Brill Building, the hit factory of the '50s and '60s. Every floor was buckling beneath the weight of musicians, producers, artists, engineers, publishers, and songwriting teams that shaped and molded Top 40 radio throughout the all-too-fleeting Golden Age. Everlasting tracks like "Chapel of Love," "Will You Still Love Me Tomorrow," and "Breaking Up Is Hard to Do" were born in the Brill Building and will surely someday outlive their makers.

Myron was a stocky man and stern vocal coach, but equally warm and encouraging. His wife, Mathilda, was far less fastidious and finicky than her husband, and she would play piano while Myron focused on drawing out his student's powerful pipes. Myron coaxed Lesley into singing more with her throat and to carefully pace her breathing, rather than pelt out her voice with the force inside her chest and nasal cavity. The end result was a smoother, more relaxed sound, "classical operatic" singing that would ease itself into, and elevate, her future pop recordings.

"That's what [Lena, Ella, and Patti] were doing," Lesley told Dawn Eden in 1994. "They weren't strictly singing from the chest, or beating it out. They had lovely voices and they let them kind of just come out and ease a bit. When you grew up with the Perry Comos and the Dean Martins, what you got was this sense that it wasn't forced. Use a little finesse. Make it look easy. Make people enjoy watching it instead of thinking you're going to have a heart attack."

Myron Earnhart recognized and cultivated that quality in Lesley. He realized he would have to demand from her protesting parents more time with their daughter.

"She's got to be here *at least* twice a week," he tried persuading Ronny over the telephone.

Of course, irresolute Ronny would not be challenged, not in matters of her own children. "No. No, I'm sorry, that's impossible."

"Why?"

"Because we live in New Jersey," she snapped back. "It's just too much for me to bring her in, on top of everything else I have to do. I have a carpool—"

But Myron, who could easily match Ronny's stance and stubborn streak, persisted. "Look, if you bring her over the bridge, I'll go get her myself."

There was a short, bewildered pause from Ronny's end. "Why would you do that?"

"Because your daughter is terrific."

Sufficiently flattered, Ronny surrendered. Myron moved into the next phase of his plan; instead of their usual singing lesson, he led Lesley into a tiny recording studio in the old Ed Sullivan Theater. They passed a handful of demos onto discs—rough, raw, voice, and piano only. Lesley held onto those tunes and played them for excited friends and family.

One such family member was Lesley's cousin, Allan Albert. Allan put himself through college playing drums for a band he'd helped assemble in the Bronx. He invited his cousin to sing and goof around with the guys, which gave Lesley the opportunity to learn new material and experiment with sound and style, an environment conducive to making mistakes without pressure.

It was on a Sunday afternoon, as Allan was lounging around the Gore's home, when the phone rang. On the other end was Sal Bonafetti, the New York Italian who had founded the band. "The singer's real sick," he blurted in a panic. "What the hell are we gonna do? We can't make the wedding."

"Hold the line." Allan dropped the phone and ran to Lesley to explain the fix they were in: The group was scheduled to perform at an Italian wedding in a matter of hours, now without a lead vocalist. The cousins coupled their efforts in an attempt to convince Leo to allow Lesley to go and fill the vacancy.

Her father consented on one pivotal condition: "If she finishes her homework."

Entrusting her with Allan, who was the ripe old age of eighteen, the Gores sent the kids off to Queens. The wedding reception, in true Italian tradition, was a lavishly catered affair. Food was served in piles so deep that the tables sagged in the middle. And there was no shortage of fine spirits to wash down the platefuls of rigatoni. Lesley remembered being sat a table with her bandmates where they were forced to admire pitchers of beer and bottles of expensive wine.

On stage, the boys would play for about twenty minutes, then call Lesley up to join them. She nervously but diligently whipped out a trio of songs, then sought refuge back at the table with the rest of the boys. It was a fun and rowdy night, and in between visits to the stage, the kids became better acquainted with the pitcher of beer they'd only admired from afar. Lesley's usual Sunday night curfew was nine o'clock, right at the end of *The Ed Sullivan Show*; but that night, Lesley didn't return to Tenafly until two in the morning, having earned a cool five dollars.

It was an unexpected but wonderful lesson in holding an audience, moving seamlessly from one song into another. Nearly five hours had gone by before the young singer realized her concentration had been entirely absorbed in what she was doing, enjoying and honing the moments.

She appeared with the band a month later at New York's Prince George Hotel. Sal Bonafetti was on a mission to get his group some representation and, hopefully, a solid record contract. In the audience were people of varying levels of importance from the music industry. Lesley, who cousin Allan had invited to tag along, performed a pair of songs herself. Her voice—heavy with natural talent and nourished training—filled every open space in the hotel lounge, piercing the ears and whetting the interest of Irving Green, the president of Mercury Records, seated only a few rows away from the girl who would soon become the most famous teenager on Earth.

So close to record executives, Allan set the sixteen-year-old's demos on a pathway that quickly resulted in his cousin's superstardom. He gave the recordings to his brother, Howard, who, as a hobby, managed prizefighters. An ardent boxing fan, Howard Albert was in charge of handling welterweight champion Emmiel Griffith. Howard gave Lesley's songs to Griffith's agent, Joe Glaser, who had also represented fighter Louis Armstrong; Glaser himself had become one of the most well-respected forces in the entertainment industry. Glaser was immediately impressed by Lesley's voice and passed her along to his best buddy, label president Irving Green, over at Mercury. At one of Mercury's monthly meetings, Green passed along the demo to a group of A&R reps, who all passed, except for one—an up-and-coming music producer, Quincy Jones.

# LET'S GET THIS PARTY STARTED

Even moguls, seemingly born fully grown and brimming with greatness, have humble beginnings. Quincy Jones was born in Chicago, Illinois, on March 14, 1933. Soon after he arrived, the family settled in Seattle, Washington, where he learned to play trumpet, piano, and even sang in a gospel quartet. Knowing that music was his calling, Jones enrolled in the prestigious Berklee College of Music in Boston.

Before he could graduate, Jones was recruited by Lionel Hampton to play trumpet in his band, and the excited young musician leaped at the chance to tour. The experience taught him more about musical arrangements, and by the '50s he was arranging for, and helping guide the lustrous careers of, the best in the business: Ray Charles, Duke Ellington, Sarah Vaughan, and the revved-up LaVern Baker.

Over the next four decades, Quincy Jones would use his masterful skills to produce records, promote major talents, score major motion pictures, establish his own record label called Qwest, and prove his own mettle as an artist (he would collect half a dozen Top 40 singles, the biggest being the #14 hit, "One Hundred Ways"). Of course, Jones would be responsible for the outstanding production of Michael Jackson's most sensational albums, *Off the Wall*, *Thriller*, and *Bad*. Overall, Jones earned an Emmy Award for his original music on the TV miniseries *Roots*; seven Academy Award nominations for dramatic film scores; and, out of seventy-nine Grammy nods, brought home twenty-seven of them to adorn his mantle.

In 1961, Clyde Otis—the first African-American artist and repertoire man for a substantial label—left his post at Mercury Records wide open for Jones's taking. The company had been spending most of its time, money, and effort pushing "serious" artists like Sarah Vaughan. But Jones watched adolescent buyers cram into record stores to sweep up records by the Shirelles, Frankie Avalon, and the Everly Brothers, all on rival labels. He told Mercury president Irving Green that they needed to tap into the teen market wealth, and fast.

Contrary to rumors that Quincy chose Lesley on a bet that he could build a pop star out of an average teen (uncannily reminiscent of Lesley's beloved Eliza Doolittle), he listened to Lesley's amateur demos and knew he'd found his vessel into the pop charts with this sixteen-year-old Jewish girl.

Over the years, Jones was fond of saying that he had met Lesley's voice before he had ever met her in person. She had an instantly recognizable voice, which Jones knew was good for radio, but more than that he was impressed by the youngster's jazz singer sensibilities, the way she could easily bend and shape a lyric. And she could sing on key, which a lot of the early kids on 45 struggled to do.

Lesley was invited up to his Fifth Avenue office in Manhattan. Lesley remembers him as a "big kid," and was moved by the care and genuine interest he showed in her as a budding musician. The pair spent the next couple of days tinkering at the piano, allowing the producer to hear, in person, the chapel bell clarity of his ingénue. When they finished, Jones looked her in the eyes and asked warmly, "Would you like to record a few sides?"

Lesley politely accepted.

Ronny Gore would later confess that she was horrified by the idea of her daughter becoming a recording artist. She and Leo had heard the stories that swirled around their favorite stars of the '40s and '50s, with the stigmas of boozing, philandering, long hours working, long months touring, and—most terrifying—the tragic ends that had already claimed the lives of Buddy Holly, Patsy Cline, and Jim Reeves. Show business was a world away from where they wanted their daughter to be.

Despite their initial objections, the Gores knew that the chances of this whole singing "thing" taking off were very slim, with an even higher possibility of the whole process being ditched entirely. "It'll never happen," a close family friend said to Ronny one afternoon.

"She'll never forgive you if you don't at least let her try. Look, the chances of her becoming a star are a million to one."

So, hoping their little girl would quickly get past this fad and go to school, marry a nice young man, and settle down in the suburbs of Jersey near her mother, the Gores strapped on their poker faces and welcomed Quincy Jones to their home in February 1963. He arrived with no small pomp and circumstance; having never learned to drive, he pulled up in a chauffeured limousine and anxious neighbors watched as a black man popped up on their quiet Tenafly street. He enlisted the aid of the family to help him carry in two huge boxes containing two hundred demos for Lesley to sample. They set up shop in the den, and Leo and Ronny, keeping their reservations to themselves, watched as Jones used rock 'n' roll to seduce their daughter into the shadowy world of show people.

Lesley spent the rest of the day skimming all two hundred records. Jones had personally auditioned every song prior to his visit, and instinct told him which one should go on top of the stack. As cleverly planned, Lesley listened to a little number called "It's My Party" first.

"Hey, I like that one," Lesley said, once the track was over. "Let's put this one in the 'maybe' pile."

By the bottom of the second box, "It's My Party" was the only song that had survived Lesley's scavenging. There was something special in the song that she could relate to as a teenage girl, just as Jones had rightly predicted.

Although Lesley was more than ready to set the song to vinyl, Jones needed more time to find a few more suitable tunes to complete a formal recording session. Heartthrob Paul Anka, the pop mainstay behind immortal classics "Diana" and "Put Your Head On My Shoulder," rose to the occasion and provided Jones with the raucous "Hello Young Lover" and the tamer, lovelorn "Danny." To make it an even four sides, Jones settled on "Something Wonderful" from the Rodgers and Hammerstein musical, *The King and I*. With the songs picked and the musicians rehearsed, Lesley Gore entered the Bell Sound Studios in New York City at two o'clock in the afternoon on Saturday, March 30, 1963, on the verge of creating her own American classic.

When the doors shut behind her, the New York reality was outside, while something much more surreal unfolded in front of her. There were so many people in the room, Lesley would tell Fred Bronson in a 1996 interview that she "couldn't figure out what they needed me for." The floor was teeming with musicians, the whole orchestra organized neatly beneath two overhead microphones. Piano players shuffled their sheet music into place as the brass section riffed scales on their horns. Against an opposite wall, a dozen men and women gathered around a single mic to sing backup.

Jones appeared from the crowd and greeted the Gores. He gently draped an arm around Lesley and said, "You come with me, Little Bits." In that moment, his nickname for her was christened and lasted through their decades-long friendship ("But you have to be really careful how you pronounce it," Lesley would often joke in her live performances).

Her parents watched with trepidation. Ronny watched helplessly as Lesley was steered away from her and sealed in a booth, though the teenager—equipped with headphones, a pencil behind her ear, and a bottle of Coca-Cola—proceeded with confidence. "I was so nervous about all this," Ronny explained to this author. "But I figured if I let her do this, it's out of her system."

The producer made sure to review the score with the singer, explaining the song to her measure by measure, note by note. Once he covered the semantics, he pointed to the top of the page and said, "Here you are. You're the lead vocalist, okay?"

Jones left her alone and returned to the technicians' booth to join engineer Phil Ramone and the music arranger, Claus Ogerman. The studio fell into dead silence, then exploded with rhythm, handclapping, and instruments as recording began. "Danny" and the strong, resounding "Something Wonderful" were finished with relative ease. Between takes, Jones would adjust this or change that, paying close attention to details in sound and scope. He kept the young singer abreast of all his changes so that she could be included in more of the process and see it in action.

Ronny was impressed by her daughter's responsiveness. She eavesdropped as Jones gave commands through Lesley's earphones—musical directives that the teenager understood like a second language—and leaned over to Leo and whispered from the side of her mouth, "I don't know what he's talking about, do you?"

Leo smiled slightly and shook his head. "No, I don't."

But Lesley understood the game and played along. She recalled not being a secure young woman, with the usual quirks and self-consciousness of a teenage girl (one of her father's oft-quoted generational admonishments was, "Boys don't make passes at girls who wear glasses"). She found comfort in the confines of the recording booth, where the challenges she confronted were those she imposed upon herself to fine-tune her craft.

Jones had great faith in her and was anxious himself to record her single. Other young solo female artists weren't attempting the harmonies or other more complex and progressive musical elements that Lesley seemed to tackle with little effort; songs like Linda Scott's "I've Told Every Little Star" and Janie Grant's "Triangle" were both cute and popular records, but were far from complicated and sounded almost juvenile in their construction and performance.

After slicing the original seven beat introduction to "It's My Party" to just two trumpet blasts, the troop ran through practice twice before recording. Lesley finished singing the first verse, then gazed out the studio window at the street outside, believing the orchestra was in the middle of the instrumental break. Sipping some Coke, the music suddenly stopped and Jones intoned over the speakers, "Little Bits, you just swallowed the second verse."

They started from the top again, and Lesley spoke of the pressure-free environment to Dawn Eden, saying, "If you didn't like it, you could do it over again. So it gave a lot of latitude, and it was very challenging. Quincy really showed me what it was to get in there and challenge yourself, to listen to something and see if you could do it better."

By five o'clock, "It's My Party" was on tape and the Gores were thanked and ushered out of the building. The teenager from Tenafly was reeling from those hectic, hurricane three hours, and though it left her upside down, she was thrilled.

Later that same night, Lesley went to the movies with her girl-friends while Quincy Jones had business to attend to. Representing Mercury Records, he went to Carnegie Hall to host French singer Charles Aznavour in concert. On the front steps of the gorgeous theater, a race was begun by an unintentional shot in the dark.

A limo pulled up to the curb and deposited Phil Spector, the twenty-three-year-old genius producer who worked every piece of an orchestra, galloping drum lines and fierce castanets into his songs to create the lush, mushy "Wall of Sound" that characterized his label. Tapping into the ignored, bountiful pool of girl groups, Spector was building a name for himself and placed the Crystals, the Ronettes, and the Paris Sisters, among many delightful dolls, at the top of the charts. His brilliance was matched by his eccentric-ity—it was rumored he listened to a single note thirty times before mixing its perfect pitch, and he was known to carry a handgun everywhere he went in paranoid concern for his life.

"Quincy!" Spector swooped in, his redlined cape bellowing out behind him like a vampire's cloak. "Quincy, I just recorded the greatest single I've ever heard, and remember me saying this to you tonight, it's going to be a *smash*."

Unfazed by the contender, Jones casually asked what the song was.

Spector replied victoriously, "'It's My Party.'"

It instantly dawned on Jones what had, up to that point, been unknown to everyone involved—the music publisher had promised the "exclusive" track to three different buyers. Before Spector and Jones had even snatched it up, "It's My Party" had already been re-corded once before by Helen Shapiro. Fortunately, her uninspiring version was used as filler on her European-released LP, and so the very first recorded "It's My Party" has since become a rock relic.

Jones had to act fast. The Crystals had just come off the colossal back-to-back successes of their #11 hit, "He's Sure the Boy I Love" and their #1 monster, "He's a Rebel" (which Spector frantically released before Vicki Carr could beat him to it), and had only recently completed the surefire hit, "Da Doo Ron Ron" that would go on to propel the girls into the #3 spot on the charts. Jones was certain, under Spector's remarkable direction and Lala Brooks' dynamite voice, that the Crystals could easily ride "Party" well into the top spot before Lesley's cut would even see the glow of a Wurlitzer jukebox.

Jones could not sit through the concert at Carnegie Hall. He had to move. He dashed out of the theater, giving only quick obligatory greeting to Charles and to colleagues while rudely ignoring others in his haste to his car. He called up engineer Phil Ramone and alerted him to Spector's arrangement, then stopped by the dark and lonely Bell Studios to pick up the master tape, still cooling from hours before.

Early Sunday morning, a sleepy Phil Ramone met Jones at nearby A&R Studios where they spent most of the day making copies of the song, eventually pressing a hundred records on their own. "I was exhausted," Ramone laughed to this author, "but Quincy knew we were running out of time and had to act fast, or we'd lose this opportunity for good." The next morning, Monday, the discs were mailed off to the largest radio stations across the nation. By Wednesday, "It's My Party" was already gaining tremendous airplay.

New York disc jockey "Cousin" Brucie Morrow, then a leading personality on WABC, gave the 45 a whirl, and the phones around him suddenly fired up like bottle rockets. His initial reaction was that he'd said something naughty on the air (the feisty radio host often had to watch his comments once the mic was hot). Afraid of a reprimand from some thoughtless on-air quip, Morrow nervously picked up the lines. There came, instead, a tsunami of inquisitive young callers:

"Hey, can you play that again?"

"What was that song?"

"Who's that by?"

"Who's that girl?"

"Where does she come from?"

"*Please*, can you play that one more time?"

"She's a homegrown kid," the overwhelmed deejay replied. "She's a Jersey girl." After that revelation, the song obliterated the competition in the Northeast. One radio station in Pittsburgh was forced to play the single several times every hour over several hours, just to meet the demand of requests that deluged the station's call center.

Only five days after it had been recorded, Lesley was driving home from school to start the weekend when she heard herself on WINS radio for the very first time. Initially, she wasn't sure it was her own voice and thought, for a moment, it wasn't her after all. After a few more measures of the song, she reconciled the sound coming out of her tiny car speakers with the enormous sound she remembered hearing in the studio; listening more closely, she sang along and found she could match every inflection. Hardly able to drive, she screeched to a stop in front of a friend's house in Englewood Cliffs, spun the volume knob way up, and ran screaming to the front door. "It wasn't an overnight success," Lesley joked during a live performance in Palm Springs. "It was more like a few days."

"I was amazed at how quickly that song hit," Phil Ramone told this author. "At one point, I think we were selling something like ten- or twenty-thousand of those things a day. I was just a kid myself then, and I hadn't been a part of that kind of success before."

Nationally, the song was picking up momentum. It entered the charts around May 11 at #60, a week after Lesley's seventeenth birthday. She knew of the record's regional success (after a deejay referred to her on air as "the sweetie pie from Tenafly," fans started to camp out on the front lawn of her home and place telephone calls to the Gore residence to speak to the singer), but had no idea of its blanket cover over Los Angeles, San Francisco, and Seattle. By the second week of its release, the song made a nomadic move from its sixtieth place to twenty-sixth, then bounded to #9.

Despite the climb in the charts, Jones was leery of Lesley's name. "Gore" was too harsh, almost violent. He suggested that he, Phil Ramone, and Irving Green come up with a new, more delicate stage name. The crew brainstormed over what to call their artist while Jones jetted off to Japan for three weeks. Halfway into his trip, he called Mercury and asked Green, "How are we doing with the name?"

"You haven't heard, have you?" Green said coyly.

"What's going on?"

"The record's number one," Green replied. "How do you like her name now?"

"Fine," Jones said. "It's fine."

## Track Three

# TEARS ON MY PILLOW

Certain songs are natural-born smash hits. "Leader of the Pack" by the Shangri-Las, "The Lion Sleeps Tonight" by the Tokens, and "Baby Love" by the Supremes were inevitable. All the right players conjoined at just the right time with just the right song to produce a record that couldn't be anything less than a blockbuster. Faster than Motor City could build a Buick—less than sixty days after her session at Bell Studios—"It's My Party" rocked out of every teenager's Dansette and topped the US pop chart, the R&B chart, and cracked England's conservative Top 10.

The simplest, most arcane piece of happenstance can lead to the creation of something phenomenal. "Angel Baby" was a heartfelt poem that a lovesick fifteen-year-old Rosie Hamlin wrote for her first boyfriend, and "My Boyfriend's Back" wouldn't have made vinyl if its songwriter hadn't overheard a girl at a soda fountain scream the sentiments of the title to a letch trying to put the moves on her in her boyfriend's absence. "It's My Party" has its roots in a tantrum that teenager Judy Gottlieb threw when her parents forced her to invite her grandparents to her high school birthday party. When her father, Seymour, implored his daughter to stop crying, bratty Judy bawled back, "It's my party, and I'll cry if I want to!" Judy's accidentally catchy phrase sparked a song idea for her father, who, in the lighthearted spirit of revenge that only a parent can dole out, made his daughter Judy the villain of the song's narrative. Gottlieb shared the bit of sketchy lyrics with his friend and songwriting partner, Herb Wiener.

While watching horses thunder their way around a racetrack, Wiener, enthusiastic with the song's potential, was distracted by the refrain and couldn't stop obsessing over the story that was emerging about a birthday party ending in a dramatic teenage showdown. He

**TOP 10 SINGLES
MAY 1963***

#1  It's My Party
    Lesley Gore

#2  Sukiyaki
    Kyu Sakamoto

#3  You Can't Sit Down
    The Dovells

#4  Da Doo Ron Ron
    The Crystals

#5  I Love You Because
    Al Martino

#6  Those Lazy-Hazy-Crazy
    Days of Summer
    Nat "King" Cole

#7  Hello Stranger
    Barbara Lewis

#8  Blue on Blue
    Bobby Vinton

#9  Still
    Bill Anderson

#10 If You Wanna Be Happy
    Jimmy Soul

*From Dave McAleer's *Book of
Hit Singles*

called his friend, composer John Gluck Jr., in the middle of the night. Gluck had made musical popcorn with the two Bobbys (Vee's "Punish Her" and Vinton's "Trouble Is My Middle Name"), and he immediately set Wiener's chorus to melody. The next day the duo played their unfinished concoction for publisher Aaron Schroder. Schroder liked the sampling and recommended songwriter Wally Gold to help out with the missing verses; Gold co-wrote "Half Heaven-Half Heartache" for Gene Pitney and "Good Luck Charm" for the King himself. The boys locked their door and sat up all night hammering out the final lyrics and melody to their certain smash.

By the summer of 1963, most everyone in the world knew the harrowing saga of Lesley, her cheating boyfriend Johnny, and that gal-pal-turned-jezebel Judy. Johnny and Judy have left Lesley's party, brazenly hand in hand. Our heroine refuses to dance or even bother feigning a good time, and to add devastating insult to injury, the pair of scoundrels return to the house so that Judy can show off Johnny's sacred high school ring. The lyrics suggest a more subversive scandal in what the song fails to illicitly describe—where had the pair disappeared to, and what were they doing? Lesley has no choice but to weep, and since it's her birthday, she'll do what she damn well pleases. Furthermore, she is absolutely certain that we would cry, too, if such misfortune should befall us.

The love triangle was set to a rousing, Latin-tinged beat, replete with hand clapping and blaring horns. The production standards were impeccable, even charming with the slight errors that mark the innocence of the day—like the trumpets that sputter out of sync; the male background singer whose voice grows unintentionally louder than the others; and the single, accidental stray handclap at the end of the instrumental break. "But those were the kinds of things that made those records special," Lesley explained to Fred Bronson, "that they weren't necessarily letter perfect."

What was nearly perfect was the polished, professional image Lesley debuted to the world. Without a doubt, the teenager was a beauty—barely five feet tall, slim (not quite a hundred pounds and only a size four-and-a-half shoe), with soft but regal European features, chestnut hair, and luminescent, almost transparent green eyes.

Her wardrobe suggested she meant business; while publicity stills of the Angels and the Chiffons show the girls in poofy, flowery bridesmaid-style gowns, Lesley adopted a decidedly more sophisticated look, a tailored, conservative couture. "She was a serious artist," fellow girl-group songbird Ronnie Spector would later say in a statement to the *Washington Post*. "She was way ahead of her time." The refined slacks-and-suits image inspired Jean Linehauser, then the head of Mercury's publicity department, to foster the singer's reputation as the poor little rich girl. That reputation was created—and stuck like a curse—when Lesley spent her birthday weekend in Detroit to appear on a local dance show. The family was waiting for Lesley's cue in the colonial-style TV studio that resembled an exclusive ski lodge. As Lesley explained to Dawn Eden, "My father was sitting in the lobby in front of a very large fireplace, and so they had me stand next to him and take some pictures. The station also had a big driveway, and they sent a limousine to pick us up. So, suddenly, I look in a teen magazine and this became 'my house,' and here was my father and I in 'our den.' So the wealthy image always felt a little uncomfortable for me." Though the public was led to believe that Lesley was a daughter of fortune, her parents had to save up for the constant round-trip taxi fare for Lesley's music lessons just a few scant months earlier.

Morris Diamond, the label's director of national promotion, recalled a conversation he had with Leo regarding travel arrangements for the Gores to attend a record hop in Ohio. Diamond had purchased budget airline tickets to save a few bucks, but Leo told him, "Morris, it's been thirty years since any of my family or I have traveled coach, and we're not about to start now. Would you please organize the proper tickets for us?" Though on its surface the tone could be misconstrued as elitist, it was the request of a proud man who worked hard to provide for his family and refused to compromise on the lifestyle he had strived to create for his wife and children.

Later, when she began touring during school breaks and recesses, Lesley grew even more resentful of the posh, haughty image Mercury had manufactured for her, as labelmates and other performers avoided her, believing she would look down on them. "You can't imagine how terrible I felt when I would walk past open dressing rooms and see them filled with people having fun," she lamented in a 1964 magazine article called "No Invitation for Lesley Gore." "I felt myself blushing and hoping someone would invite me in, and they were wondering why I didn't just walk in." Singer Bobby Rydell, who enjoyed a string of hits like "Wild One" and "Forget Him," as well as a starring role in the film version of *Bye Bye Birdie*, thought that Gore was "one of those oh-so-distant rich girls who just can't be bothered," but the ice thawed between them when he discovered with surprise that Lesley, indeed, had a sense of humor. Lesley also remembered a day after school when she heard her little brother lecturing a classmate on the phone, "She's not a snob, she's shy." Heartthrob Lou Christie, who'd scored a national hit the year before with "The Gypsy Cried," made a similar observation to the *Examiner* about meeting the introverted singer: "Lesley was a protected new star who seemed way above it all until you had some time alone with her. She was fun, smart, and talented, with a sense of humor that was her secret glory." Lesley's family and close circle of friends at the Dwight School for Girls knew the real working-class girl, but that tiny, exclusive circle was shrinking as the engineered reputation she defended herself against in nearly every interview took hold and defined the mythological Lesley Gore on album covers.

Also conveniently discounted was Lesley's Jewish heritage. Even after the celebrations following World War II had subsided and the tickertape was swept off the streets, there remained in certain parts of the United States a virulent dose of anti-Semitism. Besides, high school audiences didn't care for heavy conversations on politics or religion; teen magazines listed the interests, hobbies, and romantic daydreams of the stars, ignoring enlightening cultural differences in favor of presenting teen idols as having formed from the same bland, shallow mold. As an adult, Gore would reflect on the place and value of religion in her life when she told writer Denise Penn, "I was brought up in the Jewish religion, and I do observe certain holidays when I can. There are times when I am working, and I don't let my work interfere with a religious occasion. But I think of myself more as a spiritual person. I believe that I have a higher power and that the higher power is in myself. I believe that if you do good in this world, that comes back to you."

And of course, there was the hair.

Lesley's characteristic flip, neatly parted, impenetrable, with ends rolled up as solid as soup cans. Also adorned by Marlo Thomas, Mary Tyler Moore, and First Lady Jackie Kennedy, Lesley took the hairspray sculpture to new extremes. One windy day in Chicago, the gusts were so strong that pedestrians along State Street had to pull themselves along the metal bars that run parallel with the boulevards; nevertheless, Lesley's hairdo remained perfectly intact. "It never moved," she often joked.

With sudden fame and her public persona firmly intact, Lesley was ready to record again to prove she wasn't a one-hit wonder who would be easily shoved aside to make room for the next bubbly female singer. Legend dictates that following the stunning success of "It's My Party," Ronny Gore, now not so cold to the idea of Lesley's entertainment career, blew into Jones's office in a luxurious fur coat, perched herself atop his radiator and, with Joan Crawford-esque flare, told the producer, "Make my daughter a star!"

On May 14, three days after her freshman single wiped out all the competition, Quincy Jones brought Lesley back into the studio to record "Judy's Turn to Cry." Written by Beverly Ross and Edna

Lewis, the sequel to "It's My Party" continued the melodrama of the star-crossed young lovers. When Lesley kisses some boy at a new party, Johnny flies into a jealous rage and sucker punches the poor schmuck, proving once and for all that his heart belongs to only one girl—and that bitch Judy gets her very just desserts.

Years later, the singer would admit that the idea of a sequel was "nerdy" to her, and she would have rejected the song outright if she'd known it would become a signature Gore tune. After mulling the lyrics over, she relented and decided to move forward with the recording, intrigued by both the continuing story established in its predecessor and her identification with the young characters. It was a smart move on her part; "Judy" entered the charts during the peak of another fad of early '60s music, the "answer song," by which emerging artists and rival labels tried to glom onto the resounding success of a national smash record by creating a single that continued the story arc of the original hit (the Drifters' "Save the Last Dance for Me" was answered by Damita Jo's "I'll Save the Last Dance for You," and in response to Bobby Vee's "Please Don't Ask About Barbara," Mike Regal responds passive-aggressively with "Is It True What They Say About Barbara?"). Regardless of Lesley's initial reservations to a sequel, teenagers across the continent were hungry for more of her story. The song, with an arrangement matching its predecessor, was released in June 1963, and by July, Judy had wept all the way up to #5. And Mercury Records laughed all the way to the bank.

Spurred on by the two raging hit records that had become national obsessions, Jones took a cue from "Party's" chorus and fashioned the singer's first complete album around a "cry" theme. In order to capitalize on Lesley's wild popularity, Jones forfeited fresh material to search for tear-drenched standards and classics in an attempt to save time on production. Besides the artist and the producer, arranger Claus Ogerman became a centrifugal force in the hunt for material to follow, and round off, Lesley's two monster hits.

Ogerman was paramount in designing the distinct style of the singer's tunes, and most of the titles from Lesley's Mercury catalogue, whether album filler or a single, had a crisp, clean, polished finish. Lesley described Ogerman to Dawn Eden as "a wonderful combination of science and soul," who, with his unique brand of German precision and meticulousness, knew when to double-track Lesley's voice, when to add harmonies and soaring backing vocals, but was also keenly aware of when to extract unnecessary flourishes that might distract from the message and feel of the song. Thanks to his craftsmanship, no extraneous notes or clumsy beats stood out of a Lesley Gore record like a melodic cowlick.

In only three sessions, Lesley's first full-length album, *I'll Cry If I Want To*, was completed and rushed out to stores ("We had to skirt around some pretty tight union rules back then," Phil Ramone recalled to this author. "We had to sneak Lesley into the studio after closing time to double-track her voice or lay down some harmonies to make sure we had everything done in time"). The LP was released in late June and, of the two hundred other entries clogging the pop charts, it sloshed into the #24 slot and stayed put.

The record was a much-deserved triumph, and excited fans were treated to a wider range of talent than "Party" and "Judy" were able to showcase. Among the soggy selections like "Cry" and "Cry and You Cry Alone" were a few standout tracks that allowed Lesley to shine. Her cover of "Misty," with its slow, stuttering piano, bluesy jazz organ, and beautiful Ray Charles-style backing choir, is gorgeous and very well could have held its own had it been released as a single. In her deliciously sarcastic "Cry Me a River," Lesley delivers in her best Dinah Washington deadpan one of the greatest lyrics ever— "You told me love was too plebeian." Pop writers extraordinaire Mark Barkan and Ben Raleigh contributed "Just Let Me Cry," where flowers, singing birds, and passing pairs of happy young lovers seemed to be scoffing at the singer's miserable loneliness. Also present are the bouncy Egyptian-lilting "I Would," the train-on-the-track rhythm of "What Kind of Fool Am I," and an appropriate finish with a gloomy cover of "The Party's Over."

Only a few contemporary critics sniffed at the album, calling it "contrite" and its lean, clean sound "antiseptic," but the vast majority of reviewers were supportive of the inaugural effort (one of the trades proclaimed *I'll Cry If I Want To* "The One to Watch!"). Even other recording giants took notice of the new girl on the block and became fast fans; Neil Sedaka told his author, "I admired her voice, style, and persona. I played the 45 of 'It's My Party' on my turntable over and over." And if the sales receipts from her songs weren't evidence enough of her rising star, then the imitators that followed in her wake certainly proved Lesley's debut was a monumental moment in early pop music. Labels from coast to coast rushed to release their own version of Gore—a polished, pretty young lady with a two-and-a-half-minute teen drama. Robin Ward would share a brief stint in the spotlight with "Wonderful Summer," along with Tracey Dey ("Teenage Cleopatra"), Diane Ray ("Please Don't Talk to the Lifeguard"), Debbie Dovale ("Hey Lover"), and Donna Loren ("I'm in Love with the Ticket Taker at the Bijou Movie"), while others tried to crash Lesley's party with botched birthdays of their own, like Bernadette Carole ("Happy Birthday") and Diane Renay ("Happy Birthday Broken Heart"). After "It's My Party," Andrea Carroll's "It Hurts To Be Sixteen" was a modest hit, detailing another miserable party that ends in tears—the inevitable comparisons to Lesley's song awkwardly inescapable considering Andrea was touring with Lesley just as "Sixteen" was gaining traction of its own.

And established acts simply began to copy Lesley's sound in hopes of capturing their own lightning in a bottle: The Angels had enjoyed an early hit with "Til," but would score biggest with the heavily "Party"-influenced "My Boyfriend's Back"; and Dame Connie Francis, enamored by the style and success of "It's My Party," borrowed arranger Claus Ogerman at her MGM label to record "Whatever Happened to Rosemarie" and "My Best Friend Barbara"—both sounding right at home on a Lesley Gore LP, right down to the rhythm, orchestrations, and plot elements of backstabbing girl-friends and disloyal boyfriends. But for sheer impersonation, the top prize goes to Diane Renay, whose tailored look and extraordinary vocals matched Gore's, making her the closest to what Gore would have as a rival. Renay's producer, Bob Crewe—himself an industry heavyweight like Phil Spector and Quincy Jones—sent his Gore carbon copy to the top of the charts with a brilliantly infectious ode to the maritime branch of the military, "Navy Blue," which also sounded uncomfortably close to "It's My Party." Despite their best attempts to steal the crown from Gore's throne, these one-hit wonders, according to Alan Betrock in his fantastic study *Girl Groups: Story of a Sound*, "had pretty, if nondescript voices but no roots or feel for rock 'n' roll or rhythm and blues." None of the copycats were able to generate and sustain the popularity of Lesley's records, which baffled the magicians in the industry trying to duplicate her tricks.

"It's My Party" had become so popular that even boys wanted in on the act. Kenny Chandler, the handsome teen idol who Laurie Records was grooming to be the next Dion, answered "It's My Party" with "I Can't Stand Tears at a Party," where the singer, promising a true love he'd been harboring for Lesley all along, tries to coax our dejected heroine out of her bedroom once Johnny has left the party. Chandler's song matches Gore's driving beat, uses similar chord progressions, and boasts a comparable melody and sound; but most fun of all, "I Can't Stand Tears" introduces additional characters to the newly expanded world first created in "It's My Party."

Record labels, producers, and singers weren't the only ones profiting off Lesley Gore; entrepreneurial little brother Michael began selling his big sister's autograph for fifty cents a pop.

Following the remarkable success of her singles and album, Lesley needed to make the rounds in the public forum to promote her brand, which included performing at local hops and dances (as many as twelve on a single Friday night). Her first national television appearance was with Dick Clark on his staple *American Bandstand* TV show. She was nervous and wooden, but delivered. Quincy Jones often described his awe not just of Lesley, but of the other young headliners of the Golden Age who had gone from typical teenager to teenage idol, sometimes overnight. He sympathized with the kids whose records would suddenly become national sensations, forcing the singers—often sheltered kids who had only previously performed in front of their families or high school gymnasium audiences—into the raw exposure of live or televised appearances.

To combat some of the pressure, Jones rewarded Lesley by taking her to see live performances of Lena Horne and Peggy Lee. The teenager was enthralled being in the presence of her lifelong heroes, the larger-than-life ladies right before her eyes, and Jones was pleased by the response of this apt (and rapt) pupil, who studied the ladies, their voices, and their movements.

Feeling rejuvenated and a little more relaxed, Lesley returned to the security of the studio to record what would become her third Top 5 hit in a row.

The July 1963 session yielded three songs, two of which Lesley despised and would become points of contention that would force a compromise between the artist and her handlers. The first track was "Consolation Prize," written by Gloria Shayne (who, two years earlier after a particularly brutal visit with her psychiatrist, penned James Darren's #3 smash, "Good-bye Cruel World"). "Prize" depicts a two-timing Lesley whose attempts to win back Tommy are thwarted by poor, infatuated Billy, the unsuspecting consolation prize of the title (so after all that trouble, what happened to Johnny?).

The other much-loathed song was the fantastic Barkan-Raleigh gem, "She's a Fool." Set to a foot-stomping beat, smooth harmonies, and shifting keys, Lesley's voice is at its best as she condemns the vicious girl who is mistreating the boy she knows she could love so much better if only he belonged to her instead.

Just as actors must face it in the movies, Lesley was quickly being typecast as the girl with interminable dating crises, perennially victimized, and chronically lonely. Once her "gimmick" was established, she had first dibs on any of the songs pumped out of the Brill Building offices—*as long as they matched the type*. It was generally a solid formula; following "Take Good Care of My Baby," Bobby Vee rode a crest of enormous popularity cast as *The Boy Who Stepped Aside So the Girl Could Find True Happiness with Another*; Bobby Vinton could be counted on as *The Boy Most Likely to Be Alone on a*

*Saturday Night*; and the Shangri-Las were never better than when they pelted out their epic teen tragedies after "Leader of the Pack" splattered blood and pathos on record players across the country. Though Lesley was less than pleased with her whiny role, she trusted her producer's judgment on what material was worth recording. After all, Jones was older than she was, but not as ancient and stodgy as her parents; he had his pulse on what was happening, and she knew and respected that.

He convinced her that "She's a Fool" was a dynamite tune (and he was right—despite her distaste for the song, it's simply one of the best in her repertoire). But Lesley had a proposition of her own: if she recorded "Consolation Prize" and "She's a Fool," then she got to select something else on her own, something that would speak to, and excite, her. As a result of this arrangement, Gerry Goffin and Carole King auditioned "The Old Crowd" for Lesley, and she fell in love with it on the spot. The song describes Lesley's circle of friends (the funny one, the trendy one, the smart-ass) and their adolescent good, clean times together, but she is heartbroken to see how those friendships—so rock solid in English class and at the Friday night dances—had begun to dissolve and fade away following graduation day. With Lesley herself on the verge of starting her final year of high school, "The Old Crowd" was sadly personal and has become a fan favorite over the years.

Backed with "The Old Crowd," "She's a Fool" was released in September and in no time made itself right at home in the Top 5. With a trio of megahits under her white plastic belt, she was pushed by Mercury to tour overseas with labelmates Dion ("Donna the Prima Donna"), Timi Yuro ("Hurt"), Trini Lopez ("If I Had a Hammer"), and satin-voiced Brooke Benton ("It's Just a Matter of Time"). They had all enjoyed runs on the British charts and were warmly received by zealous English fans. During their stay in London, Lesley ventured to the legendary White Elephant Club where she bumped into a quartet of mop-haired boys calling themselves the Beatles, and who were only then just gaining a following across Western Europe. According to writer Dawn Eden, "Although Lesley [did] not recall anything special about the meeting, the group must have been impressed to see her. A few months earlier, when they first heard 'It's My Party,' they had told [their] producer George Martin that they wanted their vocals to sound like Gore's—double-tracked, reverb-laden, and big."

The boys from Liverpool would use that musical innovation to smote American singers and independent songwriters when they infiltrated US borders just three months later.

Returning to the States, Lesley was scheduled to appear on the granddaddy of variety shows, *The Ed Sullivan Show*. Terrified at the prospect of performing before the largest TV audience at that time, Gore spent months prior to her appearance on the program with her face in the toilet, unsettled by the colossal exposure and the pressure to do well. Nevertheless, coming down from a major European tour, Lesley was more mature and gave a strong, dauntless performance. The singer was just thrilled that the stoic host had pronounced her name correctly, but was touched when Sullivan invited her over to him when her set was finished. A publicly emotionless man, Sullivan paid Lesley rare compliments onstage (he adored the "good girl" performers and had very little patience for brash "bad girl" groups; he would show up later as a guest of honor, along with trumpeter Dizzy Gillespie and Marilyn-Monroe lookalike Jane Morgan, at the party Mercury threw for Lesley's eighteenth birthday). Reflecting on the experience, Lesley joked to *Biography*, "So I got through my first *Ed Sullivan* without too many train wrecks."

By the end of 1963, Lesley had collected armfuls of accolades. Teen magazines across the racks named her the "Most Popular Female Vocalist of the Year," and the National Association of Record Merchants prestigiously voted her the "Most Promising Female Vocalist of 1963." At the annual Grammy Awards celebration that honors the finest in popular music, Lesley was nominated for the Most Outstanding Rock and Roll Recording with "It's My Party." Facing tough competition from Little Peggy March ("I Will Follow Him"), Sam Cooke ("Another Saturday Night"), Chet Atkins ("Teen

Scene"), and Ruby and the Romantics ("Our Day Will Come"), the coveted award went to brother-sister duo Nino Tempo and April Stevens for their humdrum cover of "Deep Purple," a surprising #1 record from November.

Her fan club, overrun with letters and requests for photos of America's most prominent sweetheart, was tirelessly helmed by president Sue Michaels, who Gore, years later, would admit was her grandmother—using a pseudonym comprised of Lesley's middle name and her brother's first name.

Around this time there were rumblings of the Beatles' upcoming appearance stateside. Of course no one could have known then how devastating their impact would be on the current music scene. When they eventually stormed our shores and filled the doorway of their airplane with their smiling faces and childish bowl haircuts, crowds screamed and wept, holding up signs proclaiming the death of the King of rock 'n' roll. The Beatles' mythical performance on *The Ed Sullivan Show* solidified their monopoly of the American pop charts. Their albums were different; they wrote and produced their own music, threading their tracks together to support a common theme. They did things their way, bucking trends to generate an unheard-of style that was uniquely their own.

Still, they were new, and like anything nobody's seen before, predictions were quickly made of their demise. The lords and ladies of the Brill Building's royal court were not yet worried, although they kept cautious eyes cast upon the lymies, just in case. After all, Gerry Goffin and Carole King had the Chiffons at the top with "One Fine Day," as did Barry Mann and Cynthia Weil with "On Broadway" for the Drifters, and Jeff Barry and Ellie Greenwich hoisted the Ronettes into the stratus with "Be My Baby." The hit factory continued to steam ahead at full throttle, as long as the Beatles didn't pose too viable a threat.

Lesley, too, was unperturbed by Paul, John, Ringo, and George that summer. One Saturday at a Catskills resort, Lesley was lounging by the swimming pool before that evening's record hop hosted by local deejay Gene Kay, when David White (of Danny and the Juniors fame) and John Madara, a pair of prolific songwriters from Philadelphia, approached Lesley outside. Armed with a guitar and a proposition, they asked her to follow them into a poolside cabana where they played for her their acoustic composition, "You Don't Own Me."

Lesley was struck by the gutsy lyrics, the sheer *nerve* of a female singer shaking her finger and commanding others not to tell her what to do or what to say. John Madara boasted with pride to the *San Luis Obispo Tribune*, "It was different for that era, a girl telling a guy off [ . . . ] That was unheard of." Thrilled by the find, she took the song to Jones's office on the Monday following the hop, and within a week the crowned Princess of Rock recorded the song that would even give the Beatles a hard day's night and a run for their money.

## Track Four

# YOU DON'T OWN ME

"I wanted to somehow break away, but there wasn't a model to show me how," Lesley told *Biography* in 2001. "I had these feelings that I didn't really know what to do with."

Musician Jim Allio astutely observed, "There was an interesting tension between Gore's marketed persona of the archetypal suburban teenage girl and the complex, angrier, and more emotionally ambivalent person who emerged in her vocals. Although at that time, Gore's flip hairdo and sunny good-girl vibe made her a welcome antidote to the teen hoodlums that hovered on the pop periphery, she was not as complicit or happy with that image as her handlers may have thought. But since her managers were her parents, outright rebellion was not immediately forthcoming."

Ellie Greenwich, an epic songwriter from the era, recalled a period when Gore struggled to attain more worthwhile material to record. Ellie befriended the singer and tried to help her make that distinction between the girl the public knew and the artist who yearned to take her music into a more substantial direction. That assertiveness, however, was not allowed to women in the era.

Growing up in the '40s and '50s, girls like Lesley absorbed the messages of a male-dominated, male-centered culture that demanded girls be silent, giving, accommodating, and coy. Nothing much was expected from young women, except becoming a wife and a mother (preferably in that order), but certainly nothing loftier than that, certainly not independence, not greatness. A 1962 Gallup poll showed American women were merely "satisfied" with their lives, and that only one in ten of the same women polled wished the same kind of life for her daughter. Even more alarming, as the poll implies, was the lack of resistance women showed to their subordinate classification. In spite of the institutional indoctrination of these social controls,

Lesley didn't subscribe to them and never quite accepted them as a conclusive philosophy. Women were beginning to squirm beneath the stifling conditions of their generation, meeting to secretly devour Betty Friedan's dangerous and provocative book, *The Feminine Mystique*, which had the audacity to ask of its female readership, *Is this all?* Even if a teenaged Lesley had only been peripherally aware of the cultural shifts happening around her, she at least had the cognizance to know that a song like "You Don't Own Me" was ripe for release. Her internal need for independence jostled in an uneasy truce against the gumdrop public persona she had to affect for business.

Lesley's own irritation with the material she believed was insipid and wimpy was confirmed by barbed judgments hurled specifically at her, hurting her all the more because, privately, she at least partially agreed with some of what the critics were saying, yet had to publicly deflect the harsh charges in defense of the label. The *Saturday Evening Post* blamed Lesley for what the periodical christened "The Dumb Sound." The *Lutheran Christian Encounter* published a treatise on female records and summarized the damaging messages contained within them, like "Things happen to me. I have no control over them and no responsibility for them," and "If love were to happen to me— *your* love—all my anxieties would be magically resolved. You, the love object, are so incomparably wonderful (in fact, divine) that I worship you and would do virtually anything to obtain you [ . . . ] If you withhold your love, or if, as fate might decree, you turn it off and give it someone else, my loneliness and anxiety become unbearable." Leaders from Catholic organizations banded together to denounce her brand of records and the sense of helplessness and anxiety the starlets emoted, and worse yet, to sermonize on the corruptible distraction of "going steady" that Gore's songs endorsed. And much to the smug bemusement of parents, the "respectable" singer Frank Sinatra famously condemned rock music as "the most brutal, ugly, desperate, vicious form of expression it has been my misfortune to hear," and Bing Crosby prematurely suggested, "Rock and roll has run its course."

Compounding Lesley's mounting frustration was the fan mail. She received thousands of letters a month since the roaring success of "It's My Party." Girls poured out their own heartaches and personal tragedies to the overwhelmed teenager to whom they felt an intrinsic connection. Raised in the bucolic, peaceful confines of Tenafly, New Jersey, an innocuous Lesley had been oblivious to the difficulties of teens mired in poverty or abuse, and the realities proved difficult but worthwhile for the young singer to wrap her head around—she marveled in an early interview about the response from fans, "There are real people out there!"

Lesley was bowed by the heavy, nearly backbreaking responsibility to those girls. Herself sick of the songs that presented her as a weak-willed, frivolous girl, Lesley insisted on making "You Don't Own Me" distinctly hers. Jones was supportive of the new project, despite the song's lyrics moving sharply away from the frothier milkshake territory Gore had laid claim to. Jones recognized her visceral need for a vocal challenge, and he obliged her, stepping aside and moving out of her way.

The song was exquisitely drafted and arranged. Set to the beat of a slow, saucy waltz, the verses are sung in a sinister minor key, while an angry, grumbling piano and a bone-clanking xylophone keep time. The percussions roll and build, and the tension finally explodes as the chorus shifts to an exhilarating major key. As Lesley demands her independence, a ghostly female choir and eerie violins—saturated in an echo chamber—waft ethereally behind her deeply double-tracked voice. Following a melancholy instrumental break, the angelic chorus repeats, and as the song fades away and the key shifts higher and higher, Lesley cries out, with ferocious intensity, for her deserved youth and freedom.

Everyone involved knew there was something different about the song, something sublime. Engineer Phil Ramone remembered the notoriously stolid, prim string section rapping their violin bows on their music stands in applause, following Lesley's astounding performance. Unforgettable, even by today's standards where almost nothing is shocking, is the juxtaposition of the song's progressive, revolutionary lyrics set against the tempo of an archaic, classical waltz; modern listeners cannot avoid being jolted by what was doubtlessly a brave stance taken by a teenage girl singer during a time when conformity was key to survival, when the norm for a seventeen-year-old female vocalist were songs like the Crystals' "He Hit Me (It Felt Like a Kiss)," or the Fabulettes' "Try the Worryin' Way," in which the singer insists that the best way for a girl to shed a few extra pounds (to attract a man) is by falling in love with a boy she can't trust, or Ginny Arnell's atrocious "Dumb Head," which includes, among other sickening lines, "I'm a dumb head / Just a stupid little girl with a peanut for a brain."

> **TOP 10 SINGLES**
> **FEBRUARY 1964\***
>
> #1  I Want To Hold Your Hand
>      The Beatles
>
> #2  You Don't Own Me
>      Lesley Gore
>
> #3  Um, Um, Um, Um, Um, Um
>      Major Lance
>
> #4  She Loves You
>      The Beatles
>
> #5  Out Of Limits
>      The Marketts
>
> #6  Hey Little Cobra
>      The Rip Chords
>
> #7  Java
>      Al Hirt
>
> #8  For You
>      Rick Nelson
>
> #9  Dawn (Go Away)
>      Four Seasons
>
> #10  Anyone Who Had
>       a Heart
>       Dionne Warwick
>
> \*From Dave McAleer's *Book of Hit Singles*

"You Don't Own Me" was unleashed on an unsuspecting public in December and soared to #13. Rock deejay Brucie Morrow had adored the young star since her debut single and had been booking her on his weekend music shows. When "You Don't Own Me" was released, Morrow immediately led the charge for support of the record, dismissing any hesitation by other radio programmers to promote the radical song. Morrow loved the song's revolutionary lines, and soon other skittish deejays were following his lead and spinning Lesley's defense of young girlhood on their turntables. Besides Morrow's helpful, influential professional nudges, programmers couldn't ignore the flood of requests pouring into their stations from excited fans.

Gore was taking enormous strides, with her haunting song of female emancipation charging through the masculine stampede (ironically, the song's two composers would later write the conservative "Dawn of Correction" to challenge Barry McGuire's #1 activist song, "Eve of Destruction"). This Jersey girl, an unlikely recording superstar, had achieved her fourth Top 5 single in a row, as "You Don't Own Me" filled the #2 spot in early 1964. To attract an even wider international market, Lesley recorded the song in multiple languages, helping it become a monster hit in France, Italy, and Germany (where, in the latter country, it would be renamed "Good-bye Tony" apparently to appease German censors who felt threatened by the record's stance against all male domination, so instead focused the singer's rage on a specific nasty boyfriend called Tony).

Like "Party," the popularity of "You Don't Own Me" would spur its own rash of wannabes, the strongest being Karen Kelly's "Nobody's Girl," and the most atrocious belonging to the Society Girls' single, "S.P.C.L.G. (Society for the Prevention of Cruelty to Little Girls)." One of the—um, best—imitations came from perky TV star Patty Duke, who played both halves of identical teen twins on *The Patty Duke Show*. The rock 'n' roll Patty (a hot dog makes her lose control!), like many of her young TV contemporaries, was shoved in front of a microphone to capitalize on her built-in exposure. Her first release, the most notable single among several comically unnotable singles, was "Don't Just Stand There," which soared to #8 nationally in 1965. Duke's song pulsed along to the same waltz tempo, same sinister minor key and uplifting major key shifts, same angelic background choir punctuating the drama of the song—it was even recorded in the same studio where "You Don't Own Me" was created. While the pantomiming style of "Don't Just Stand There" may have seemed like flattery to "You Don't Own Me," the message contained in Duke's song was an insult to Gore's record: Duke begs her indecisive, emotionally withdrawn boyfriend to break up with her if he's fallen out of love, but it's clear in the song that the female protagonist won't declare her own freedom from him. Instead, she relinquishes control of her own life and waits for him to make the first move, even if it will devastate her.

While it is purely conjecture and no one will ever know for sure, it seems very likely that "You Don't Own Me" could have become Lesley Gore's second #1 single, had the space not already been stolen by the Beatles and "I Want to Hold Your Hand." But Gore held on tight, even as she was ambushed from behind by the band's other massive recording, "She Loves You." Eventually the boys won out, but Lesley's groundbreaking ballad kept her in the forefront of the public's consciousness as her contemporaries, who had enjoyed hits before and beside her—like Connie Stevens, Shelley Fabares, Kathy Young, and even the titanium Shirelles—were trounced by the oncoming British Invasion and forced into musical retirement before some of them had reached drinking age.

"You Don't Own Me" was just one reason that the singer's second full-length studio album, *Lesley Gore Sings of Mixed-Up Hearts*, is superior to *I'll Cry If I Want To*. The new album, free of the restrictive novelty theme of its predecessor, showcased original material that created a broader overall sound with more diverse backing tracks, spotless harmonies and crisp, solid production values. Joined by her two latest hits, dynamic tracks like "Run, Bobby, Run," "If That's The Way You Want It," "Young and Foolish," and an early appearance of "Sunshine, Lollipops, and Rainbows" encapsulated the youthful essence of the teenage experience (the back of the album exclaims, "Seventeen! It's an enchanting age. You're just beginning to venture out and explore the world; happiness, sadness, and loneliness."). Released in November 1963, Mercury was confident that the record would parallel the chart success of *I'll Cry If I Want To* and maybe even best it.

But a tragedy greater than the British Invasion would take place the same month that *Mixed-Up Hearts* hit record stores. President John F. Kennedy was gunned down on November 22 as his motorcade wound through the streets of Dealey Plaza in Dallas, Texas. The assassination of a sitting president was thought to be unheard of in modern America, something that only happened in textbooks, something that the United States would certainly never have witnessed again after Lincoln. Deep in grief and shock, and seemingly frozen in time, Americans had no interest in beach movies, twist parties, or teen magazine celebrity profiles. By Christmas, *Mixed-Up Hearts* would reach only #51 before its rapid backslide (Gore's album would not be the only musical casualty that wretched winter; Phil Spector's superb, phenomenal classic Christmas album was released that holiday season and tanked in the pall of Kennedy's death).

Still, Lesley was proud of "You Don't Own Me," not only for its merits as a stand-alone single, but as the weapon that would bludgeon into a coma her role as the pitiful girl throwing a tantrum at a party, as the girl at the whim of a boy.

Until Quincy Jones handed her the next single.

## Track Five

# THE TROUBLE WITH BOYS

"That's the Way Boys Are," written by pop wizards Barkan and Raleigh, was released in March and became a #12 hit. The spunky song, about a cruel boyfriend whose bad behavior and wandering eye are lightly shrugged off and forgiven by the singer as simply the nature of the beast, is given a fun treatment by Lesley and company (at a live performance in the early 2000s, Lesley would joke about the song, "Boys haven't changed in forty years"); but there is a perceptible disappointment in her vocals as this song had sent her back to familiar stomping grounds—the victim. The track, nonetheless cute, depicts the singer as a girl who accepts mistreatment and minor abuses because it's easier than finding someone else. Though still a big seller, fans (and the singer alike) must have felt that the follow up to the sensational "You Don't Own Me" paled to the point of near invisibility in comparison, causing "That's the Way Boys Are" to stall at #12, and to become Lesley's first single to just graze the outside of the Top 10.

The single was backed with "That's the Way the Ball Bounces," a slow, lazy calypso that would be ideal for lounging poolside in Palm Springs with a chilled apple martini. The song is a fun exercise in '60s lounge music, aided tremendously by Lesley's relaxed and breathy delivery.

At the same time, record labels and movie studios were joining their efforts in a strategy that would return enormous profits to each side. Taking a hint (more of a shove) from the phenomenal success of Elvis Presley's movies, filmmakers used rock stars to entice the broad teen audience into theaters, while music labels and their artists capitalized on the exposure and soundtrack sales. Frankie and Annette, Connie Francis, Chubby Checker, and Joey Dee and the Starlighters twisted their way up the pop charts and surfed through impressive box-office receipts.

Mercury Records wasn't about to pass up on the opportunity to benefit from one of their most bankable stars. They lent out Lesley Gore for a cameo appearance in *Girls on the Beach*, a surf-and-turf flick that also starred the Beach Boys. Her first scene was in a beach house where she performed a rollicking little number called, "It's Gotta Be You," followed by an appearance at a beachfront hamburger joint to sing her newest tune, "I Don't Wanna Be a Loser." She pops up later on at a house party just in time to lip-sync a Lesley Gore record that one of the guests has sneaked onto the phonograph. "Leave Me Alone," penned by the singer herself, has a rousing, handclapping percussive track, and Lesley pelts it out with an assertiveness reminiscent of "You Don't Own Me."

"Leave Me Alone" is a blast of angry hot air. Lesley explained the song's dour mood to Dawn Eden, "I think I started writing it in a car on the way to a gig or something. The melody stuck in my head, and when I got home it was still there, so I transferred it to tape. I think it was very much a feeling of already being claustrophobic by fame and feeling a little closed in."

She would feel even more closed in on the set of the movie—quite literally, as she was quarantined. Her scenes had been completed by noon, but by one o'clock her face and neck were covered in a bright red rash. Two hours later, she was racked by fever and nearly had to be hospitalized. She was diagnosed with German measles, and she had passed it along to everyone else on the set. "I don't think they'll *ever* forget me," she laughed, in the same interview.

Fortunately, the crew recovered and *Girls on the Beach* was released and saw moderate returns. Taking advantage of the film's popularity, Mercury began promoting Lesley's sixth single, "I Don't Wanna Be a Loser." The earnest outing couldn't match the spunk of her previous titles, and the record stumbled into #37—now the farthest away a Lesley Gore single had fallen from the Top 10.

Still, riding hot on the heels of a motion picture appearance and a single in the precious Top 40, the label released Lesley's third studio album in May 1964. *Boys, Boys, Boys* scored almost as well as her debut, holding fast at #39. The LP boasted her latest two singles, both songs featured in the film, two of her original demo recordings, and a few more nuggets: Paul Anka pitched in "Boys," and Lesley contributed her own "I'm Coolin', No Foolin'," a moody, unsettling tune where our heroine attempts to steel herself against the advances of a persuasive young man.

Despite the boy-fixated concept of the album (the cover depicts a grinning Lesley Gore in front of a wall of male names including Amos, Con, and Seymour), songwriters John Madara and David White—the founding fathers of "You Don't Own Me"—wrote the sound-alike "Don't Call Me (I'll Call You)," which is also the album's standout track. Set to the same undulating waltz as its predecessor, "Don't Call Me" repeats the familiar pattern of minor key verses that burst into climactic major keys. Lesley's vocal kickboxing was as assertive and sincere as it was on "You Don't Own Me," but the song's obvious similarity to the earlier hit, as well as the riptide of imitators left in its wake, kept it from being released as a potential single.

With the release of *Boys, Boys, Boys*, there was no doubt that the eighteen-year-old singer was a superstar. The high school senior enjoyed a trio of popular albums and half a dozen singles, most of them having stared down from their firm perch in the Top 10, and none of them outside the Top 40. As her producer scrambled to press, distribute, and promote the next big smash, Lesley was faced with a much harder personal decision on the home front.

Ronny and Leo had taken it for granted that their daughter would attend college. They feared that the incredible turn Lesley's life had taken would keep her from going beyond the twelfth grade. "Look," she assured her parents, "I promise you that I'm going to college, if I hit with the next record or not." Her parents had little to worry about, as comments she made in magazine interviews in the mid-'60s were more urbane and articulate than the typical teen idol rubbish. "All the success in the world can't replace an education," the poised celebrity stated in a fan magazine. "I want to develop my ideas intelligently and then live a life that will let me make this world a better place to live in."

But her decision to experience university life was not an easy one, and she questioned every move she made. A focused emphasis on her studies would curtail the steady stream of hits and perhaps damage the relationship she valued with Quincy Jones and Mercury Records, who also depended on her. And taking even the briefest hiatus from music was a shaky option, as Lesley explained to Dawn Eden that "the same career would not be out there when I finished in four years."

If the executives at Mercury were upset with their star's choice to escape the rigors of recording and performing, they didn't show it. They gritted their teeth and wished her well as she gathered her books and passed through the ivory towers of Sarah Lawrence College in Bronxsville, New York. She had graduated high school with honors and was looking forward to the respite and solace that the private college would offer—and, as one could expect of a young woman who recorded "You Don't Own Me" with conviction and truth, Gore's decision to attend university marked her own individuality and independence. "It did afford me a way of being able to back out a little and get some perspective on the whole [fame] thing," she recalled to Dawn Eden. "I really did have the sense that if I continued with my career, I would never go back to school." The liberal arts college, with its focus on the performing arts and humanities, was an ideal fit for Lesley, who loved literature, poetry, and writing. The all-girl campus (the school would not go coed until that radically transformative year, 1968) gave her a sense of familiarity and a place in which to relax from the strain of celebrity, although the transition would not be a completely smooth one.

To appease Irving Green, Quincy Jones, and the other gods at Mercury, Lesley continued to fit in recording sessions and make personal appearances to both honor her contract and keep her name on the public radar. This meant squeezing performances into summer vacations, holiday breaks, and recesses between semesters; it was taxing on the student, and her handlers were less than pleased that they couldn't wring as much out of her as they wanted. Jones conceded to Lesley's obstinate arrangement. Privately, Jones must have been upset to be losing the musical momentum of one of the label's most profitable stars.

On campus, students and professors had to force themselves not to become distracted by the star in their midst. Intimidated, classmates veered away—and girls who were bolder were determined to deflate the singer's falsely perceived ego. Passing Lesley in a dormitory hallway, a student leered at her: "I didn't know you were *that* short." Lesley gamely laughed it off, but it would mark the first of many biting interactions by classmates who were in awe—and resentful—of her celebrity status and falsely suspicious of the notion that her arrival on campus was merely a publicity stunt for the bubbly star ("I got through my years at Sarah Lawrence on 'cute,'" the singer joked to Edward Eckstine in 1976). Dirty looks, whispered gossip, and cold shoulders greeted her in the quads and cafeterias. Her records had fallen from favor with the college group, whose tastes had evolved with folk music and British mod fashions. In a further attempt to fit in like anyone else, Gore told a fan magazine in 1965, "I love dancing. The frug and the jerk and the shing-a-ling are a real groove." Her public comments about college life were charitable and optimistic, but privately, according to writer Sheila Burgel, she complained that her classmates treated her "like shit."

"She was sweet and shy, not stuck up," remembered one former, kinder classmate to *Althouse*. "Her fame and music were never discussed. She was unique at Sarah Lawrence at the time as the only student with a personal bodyguard." Another woman added, "I remember her being followed by a guard from class to class, but other than that, she seemed like any of the other girls." Still another former graduate offered, "I don't remember anything unusual or pretentious standing out about her, which I guess is exactly what she was hoping for."

She managed to forge a couple of shaky friendships with her roommates, but was wise enough to keep them at bay until they built mutual trust with one another. By the holidays, Gore felt confident enough to join the Freshman Follies, which was written and performed by first-year students. She appeared in a skit that lampooned her professional image—her character was a clumsy ballerina who, after a disastrous rehearsal akin to a scene in *I Love Lucy*, is thrown out of the dance studio, only to have the others onstage, including the ballet instructor, drop their own formal airs and start dancing around to a recording of "It's My Party." Students began to relax around her, seeing that she could skewer her own reputation with tongue firmly planted in cheek. "The other girls saw that Lesley the girl and Lesley the singer were just flip sides of the same personality," Lesley wrote in a late-60s article about her college experience.

Away from the regimented life at Tenafly and decompressing from the constant responsibilities to Mercury, Lesley was allowed to develop another facet of that personality, to explore and validate a part of herself she fiercely protected from the glare of the spotlight. Fans only knew the Lesley who pined in her songs for Johnny or Bobby or Danny; the lovelorn Lesley in black-and-white stills holding a telephone to her ear and sighing into the receiver; the Lesley whose infatuation with boys—the good guys and the guys who abused her—made her every girl's best pal. Now, relishing in newfound freedom away from routine and clinging to the privacy afforded her at college, a fully realized composite of Lesley Gore was emerging that, made public, might destroy her career forever.

Gay Americans in the early '60s had no visibility, no representation, no allies to protect their identities. They were often the targets of witch hunts, police harassment, and random acts of brutality. Homosexuality was an offense to the norm, forcing gays and lesbians to remain in the darkness, secrecy, and even security of their tightly bolted closets. The America that celebrated Lesley Gore—the society that held her up as a paragon of virtue, manners, and civility for her young fans—would never have accepted anything outside of the parameters of comfort and tastefulness, forcing Lesley, who was only just starting to make discoveries of her own sexual identity, to hold her silence rather than face rejection or humiliation. It would be a few years before Gore would wholly accept and embrace being gay, but the escape to Sarah Lawrence, and the opportunity to develop a personality and sense of self separate from the gauzy album covers, allowed her to question herself, and permitted the possibility to form the woman she would mature into.

"I just experimented with boys and girls and had reason to adore them both," Lesley explained to Denise Penn in 2006. "I think my first really serious relationship was a gay one, so that began to tell me things about myself."

Discretion was key, but keeping up appearances was even more paramount. Her parents, in keeping with the conventions of the time, were expecting their daughter to meet a nice man, marry, and have children; and Lesley, with her albatross of fame, couldn't put on the dark jeans and leather jackets like her older female friends and disappear into the night to slum it in underground gay bars. In direct opposition with the emotions and self-awareness now budding within the singer, the publicity machine at Mercury was in full throttle, promoting Lesley in ways that, as trite as they were at the time, are even more ludicrous now in sharp hindsight. The singer would attend an opening or a gala event, and the label made sure there was a man on her arm—at least for the flashbulbs (though Lesley contends that these "match-ups" were not specifically arranged to hide her sexuality, it certainly didn't hurt the orthodox image she had to posture). And one magazine spread in 1964 transcribed a hilariously contrived conversation between Lesley and Connie Francis that focused on their mutual boy troubles—doubtless, a piece of bubblegum publicity manufactured to capitalize on both ladies' enormous star power (Lesley would concede that it would be years before the ladies would finally meet). Individual publicity photos of the young women smile at one another from opposite pages, and between them is a back-and-forth exchange where Lesley picks the older Connie's brain for big-sisterly advice:

LESLEY: We might as well get right down to the "nitty-gritty"—or plain facts. What on earth does a girl do when she knows her fellow wants to kiss her goodnight, but also knows that if she does start that he will definitely lose respect for her?

CONNIE: I say she must not give in. If a guy *really* cares for a girl, he will wait till it is the right thing to do. Just think, if she doesn't kiss him, he just dumps her and goes out and tries the same trick on some other poor, innocent girl.

The fluffy, virtuous volley covers an array of topics including responding to wolf calls from boys ("I think it is well to remember that many guys who do this are flirting in a youthful and healthy manner," Lesley professes in the article), to trust, to public displays of affection, to cheating (Connie advises, "If the guy is your steady, I think you have a right to bring the matter up—speak softly, don't yell."). The insightful meeting of the minds ends with Connie offering, "What we're saying, in essence, is that the road to true love is a two-way street. We must be able to take a fellow's hand and walk beside him down that road." Lesley responds with the final line, "And if any girl thinks she can run things and tries to go out front and lead the way—well, she'll just end up walking down that road all alone."

The music Lesley produced during her college years did nothing to betray who she was developing into as a young woman. The dynamite songwriting team of Jeff Barry and Ellie Greenwich approached the singer with "Maybe I Know." The song again casts Lesley as the forlorn girl mistreated by her ever-unfaithful boyfriend. This time, though, the lyrics are darker, with Lesley neither heartbroken nor sad, but chillingly resigned. She overhears whispered gossip of her boyfriend's infidelity and how devastated she'll be once she catches on; but Lesley is already a step ahead of the crowd and knows full well he's been untrue, but clinging to her belief that he really loves her underneath it all, she resolves to keep him close until he matures and settles down, however painful the wait.

Engineer Claus Ogerman shaved off its longer introduction, opting to start the song cold turkey, with no opening bars or cues. The complicated composition—shifting between major and minor keys, a beat that pulses along to medium swing rhythm occasionally halted by a jagged shuffle—was becoming more characteristic of Lesley Gore's sound. The unique arrangement rewarded everyone involved with another hit record, and once it entered the charts in midsummer and slowly but steadily muscled its way through increasingly British pop acts, "Maybe I Know" hung on at #14 like a cat on kitchen drapes.

Quincy Jones didn't give his protégé a chance to catch her breath. With "Maybe I Know" still holding fast on the charts, the producer knew they needed to ride the wave of its success to match, or hopefully beat, the previous outing. "Let's get real," he confessed in his 2001 autobiography. "Number 1 is euphoric and addictive; numbers 2, 6, and 11 are my least favorite chart positions."

"Hey Now" was recorded and released in October and presented the singer's fans with a sound strikingly different from her other sugary discs. It was a pop record, to be sure; but the rumbling drums, groaning background singers, and Lesley's decidedly slinky, deadpan interpretation of the lyrics made it a surefire crossover contender for the rhythm-and-blues chart. As optimistic as Mercury was of the single's success, the arrangement seemed alien to either chart, causing listeners to shy away from the unLesley-like song. It fizzled at #76, her biggest flop up to that time.

Aside from the confusing topside, sales were also slowed by the record's B-side, which deejays and fans preferred. If "You Don't Own Me" was Lesley's pantheon to women's rights, then the politically appalling "Sometimes I Wish I Were a Boy" was misogynistic, if not blatantly demeaning—the usual unflattering terrain that her fans had expected from her. It managed to pick up a little airplay and anchored at the bottom of the chart at #86.

"Sometimes" has Lesley standing alone by a jukebox, sighing and pouting as boys pass her by without asking for a swing out on the dance floor. In the chorus, Lesley weakly boasts that she likes being a girl, but wishes she could be a boy in order to make the first move, as it is impolite and unfeminine to make an advance while in female form.

Recording the tune was a point of bitter debate between the producer and the disgruntled singer, who felt the song yanked her even further back from where she was struggling to be. She hated the song and affirmed later on feeling almost offended by its message, telling Dawn Eden, "I felt it was really dorky. I thought, 'I've gotten past this.'"

In exchange, Jones allowed her studio time to record whatever she wanted. Documents show that the same July recording session that produced "Hey Now" and its forgettable flipside also yielded a remake of "Secret Love," a lush and lovely standard. The sessions also included "When Sunny Gets Blue" and "You've Let Yourself Go," none of which Mercury ever believed had the potential to be singles, all of which have been lost. As writer Dawn Eden notes, "Usually such songs were done at the end of a session, either with the musicians sticking around or with Lesley just accompanying herself at the piano [ . . . ] it appears that they were just done to pacify the singer, who loved the songs and wanted very much to expand her range of styles."

Among these freestyle recordings is her cover of "Let It Be Me," which begins with Lesley singing over a muffled, bluesy bass guitar. The cabaret arrangement expands to include a lounge piano and brushed drums in a traditional slow jazz. Her voice is intense, husky, and low, sounding jarringly yet succulently adult, an homage to the great crooning ladies of the '40s and '50s that occupied the teenager's turntable at home. Had it been released as a single, her version may have been taken as seriously as a Connie Francis power ballad.

But Jones, of course, prevailed. The song was scrapped, and "Sometimes I Wish I Were a Boy" was pressed and joined the ranks of obscure novelties of that time, like Big Dee Irwin's "Happy Being Fat" and Cher's great, lost "I Love You, Ringo."

Mercury remained warmly paternal of their young charge and was determined to boost her back into the Top 10. Rather than risk another experimental song that tampered with the safe formula (and thereby restricting Lesley's growth as a more versatile performer), Jones turned to the Barry-Greenwich superteam for a more marketable composition. The writers applied their typical Midas touch with "The Look of Love," another safe and typical Gore song. The melody was refurbished with jangling sleigh bells to cash in on its winter release date; entering the charts around Thanksgiving, the undeniably catchy "Look of Love" hoisted Lesley to #27, just in time to be a holiday stocking stuffer.

The end of 1964 also saw the debut of Lesley's fourth LP, *Girl Talk*. The new album moved her away from wimpier teen fare and into the stronger, more current "girl group" subgenre which still had teeth sharp enough to bite into the Mersey sound coming into vogue; so exacerbated by the British Invasion, the author of the album's liner notes praised Gore's ability to be understood when she vocalized, an undeniable dig at the Cockney accents hiccupping across the airwaves that winter. *Girl Talk* squeaked to #85, aided by two strong singles and some of her most original, strongly delivered material and fan favorites—as well as the heavy presence of Ellie Greenwich and Jeff Barry behind the tracks. The maudlin "Little Girl Go Home" tells a story of a teenage runaway; in the bouncy "Wonder Boy," Lesley falls for a studious boy too engrossed in his schoolbooks to notice her; Dad finds a job out of town so the family is "Movin' Away," a sweet story where Lesley promises to return to the boy who misses her; plus Gore's own, "I Died Inside," replete with the clicky rhythm of a tickertape machine and chattering castanets. The standout track, though, might be the gorgeous and dramatic "You've Come Back," which celebrates the return of what was once a lost love (Gore loved the song so much that she confessed to openly sobbing the first time she heard it performed for her).

A few sluggish record sales on one stalled single couldn't down-play the fact that America simply loved Lesley. They would get to see more of their lovelorn sweetheart in a filmed concert that the kids fortunate enough to witness had no idea would become a rock 'n' roll milestone.

Before pay-per-view heralded must-see events on cable television, a revolutionary idea unfolded over two days in Santa Monica, California, in October 1964. Blending film and music each in their purest forms, executive producers William Sargent Jr. and Henry G. Saperstein gathered some of the biggest recording stars together for a concert that would be taped before a live audience at the Santa Monica Civic Auditorium, then edited together the best performances over the three-day shoot to create a phenomenal event to be played in movie houses across the country. Officially called the *Teen Award Music International Show*, it would forever be blazed into the cultural lexicon as *The TAMI Show*.

The kaleidoscopic playbill, viewed with fifty years of hindsight, is mythical: Chuck Berry, James Brown, the Rolling Stones, Marvin Gaye, the Supremes, the Beach Boys, Smokey Robinson and the Miracles, Gerry and the Pacemakers. Beach bums Jan and Dean filled the bill as hosts. Sliding, strolling, twisting, and rolling across the stage was a carousel of the most sensational artists spanning an amalgam of genres, from rock, pop, British beatniks, blues, and soul.

Striving for perfection, Sargent and Saperstein coaxed superhuman record producer Jack Nitzsche to join the project as music director. It was an ingenious coupling, and the orchestra backing the steady stream of acts was tightly tuned and conducted by capable, golden hands. Stripped of echo chambers, sound mixing, and overdubs, *The TAMI Show* was the first experiment in "unplugged" performance art, when smash hits are deconstructed to their most simplest elements—singer and song, no frills, no alternate takes. It was a radical innovation in entertainment that would influence Woodstock and Monterey Pop, which would both come to define their decade.

The crowds swarming the auditorium were so enormous that the artists couldn't escape to travel between the hotel and the venue. Instead, to save the hours that the hassle of moving back and forth would cause, the performers simply bunked at the auditorium.

The theater was filled beyond its capacity for each day of filming. The audience was mostly composed of young girls there to see the rebels they fantasized about and the pop princesses they so desperately wanted to be. From the moment a star trotted onto the stage to the moment they locomotioned off of it, the mob shrieked and squealed and clapped so ferociously that the music simply existed as ambiance; Marvin Gaye only needed to have belched and made shadow puppets, it would have elicited the same ear-bleeding reaction from the audience.

*The TAMI Show* is a time capsule, a dog-eared page in rock's history book, an electric concert that united every player by music. It also offered a glimpse of colorblindness not often seen so early in the '60s, when nearly every facet of daily living was slashed by racial lines into separate but unequal halves.

Chuck Berry and Gerry and the Pacemakers jammed together on "Maybelline," a unique merge of Old American and New British rock, an ironic clash of symbols—what rock used to be, and what it was being massacred by. Smokey Robinson & The Miracles swam and stomped in choreography impossible to describe but divine to watch. Still on the cusp of their greatness, the Supremes, led by sleepy-eyed Diana Ross sporting the tallest, heaviest beehive wig that her neck could hold, offered solid renditions of "Baby Love" and "Run, Run, Run," all the while being bombarded by distracting background dancers doing the pony. The Beach Boys jammed to their hugest hits by that time—"Surfin' USA," "I Get Around," "Surfer Girl," and "Dance, Dance, Dance." And Keith Richards of the Rolling Stones would forever lament that trying to follow James Brown's powder keg performance was the "biggest mistake" of their career.

But Lesley Gore was sent out to open the *TAMI Show* with her dynamite set, as she was, at that time, the biggest celebrity of the bunch with a bona fide string of hits already to her credit. Hosts Jan and Dean perched themselves on stools at the side of the stage. Jan chimed into the microphone, "Come on now, let's hear a roar for the sounds of Lesley Gore." The boys swiveled around on their stools to reveal Lesley's name scrawled like graffiti all over the backs of their sweaters.

The curtain of circular discs rose, and a small, dark, shadowy figure emerged into the light. At the sight of Lesley, the audience screamed so loudly that the microphones, reaching their maximum decibel levels, bristled for a moment at the noise until the crowd settled down. She immediately broke into "Maybe I Know," and signaled for the fans in the first few rows to stand up and dance.

Gore then stepped up to the center stage and the camera framed her face through a foggy, dreamlike filter. As the first angry notes of "You Don't Own Me" began, the audience silenced itself for one of the concert's most stunning moments. Her delivery was flawless, record perfect. As she flung herself into the might of the chorus, Lesley shook her fists, as if mustering up all the power in her entire tiny frame to give the song the force it deserved. The crowd erupted and didn't let up again through her next song, "You Didn't Look 'Round," where a two-timed Lesley spots her man and another girl in a dark movie theater, their indiscretions acted out just a couple of rows in front of her.

Gore next gave a happy and enthusiastic performance of "Hey Now" to boost its promotion, and the screeching audience received it warmly. But pandemonium reached its zenith when the trumpets announced "It's My Party." So overwhelmed by the deluge of cheers, Lesley had to pause during the chorus to bow and thank them, only "because the audience was so loud," she told Fred Bronson. "I couldn't hear the orchestra, and it was a *big* orchestra. They were so loud. Your eardrums almost felt like they were going to break."

To sing its sequel, "Judy's Turn to Cry," the beaded curtain rose and all the performers clapped and danced behind Lesley. The audience could not be contained; the music was smote by the cacophony, and it's no small wonder how the walls managed not to crack and collapse.

Gore recalled to *Digital Interviews* in 2002 the whirlwind moment her set on the *TAMI Show* ended. Reeling backstage, Lesley told the producers, "I have no idea what happened out there!"

As much as Lesley's public appeal had been solidified by her fifteen-minute stint on the *TAMI* concert, the '60's most famous singer was not bulletproof from criticism.

As political correctness dawned and the cause for women's rights burgeoned, feminists grew increasingly frustrated by the frivolous songs that followed the colossal "You Don't Own Me," thereby ignoring Lesley's irrefutable contribution to pop's evolution and ironically dismissing the singer's personal growth in education and her own commitment to empowering the female voice. Critics lambasted the shallowness of the lyrics, but failed to recognize the heart and brain behind them; calling Gore weak bucked the fact that no other American female singer, particularly as young as she was, was accumulating her levels of success in the tea-and-scone atmosphere of the mid-'60s. There was a striking irony between the lovesick adolescent that was presented for public consumption and the young woman struggling with her own personal identity and for more control of song content and style.

At the close of 1964 after *The TAMI Show*, producer Shelby Singleton borrowed Lesley from Quincy Jones to record nine tunes. Among them were "Teen Years," "Wasn't Loving You Enough," and a remake of the Crests' "Sixteen Candles." Of the nine tracks recorded that day, only one managed to survive the session, the rest lost or destroyed over time. "I Just Don't Know If I Can," co-written with college chum Carole Bayer, is a murky, heavily percussive Specter copycat, where the narrator is unsure how to handle a boy who can't stay true to her. She's conflicted by a love and protectiveness that seems to grow even stronger although she knows it's wrong. Finally, realizing she's wasting her time by trying to nurture a fantasy, she leaves him (albeit reluctantly), knowing she can't win a losing battle all by herself. The personal lyrics could reflect, in a sense, what was happening in Lesley's life; not able to live openly, the song spoke to the part of the young woman not able to attain the kind of love she was truly seeking.

Inexplicably, the entire session was ditched, and for all that time and effort, Mercury didn't pull a potential single out of the bunch. Even "I Just Don't Know If I Can," where the heroine chooses the painful but smarter decision to flee a failing relationship, went ignored.

Quincy Jones regained control of the helm and pressed Lesley's next single, "All of My Life," a track that the singer also adored. An upbeat love song, she's finally found the type of boy she's been searching for, going so far as to ponder marriage. It was a challenging musical arrangement, testing the range of the singer's voice in a very adult, sweeping melody. The song describes a particular love and "a special kiss"—what could be another veiled suggestion of Lesley's sexuality—and gives the singer, a hopelessly romantic Taurus, the happy ending she's been wishing for.

"All of My Life" was released in March 1965 and picked up speed in New York and New Jersey, as well as a few nods on the West Coast. But deejays didn't take to it enough to give it a chance, and diligent fans could only drag it to #71. A sad Lesley decided that the record was just too delicate an arrangement, too adult to make an impression.

On America's Independence Day in 1964, the top five slots on the American pop charts were occupied by the Beatles, but by early 1965, English acts filled a quarter of the entire chart. Groups like Herman's Hermits, Peter and Gordon, the Dave Clark Five, and Freddie and the Dreamers had made the transatlantic crossover to plow over American idols that jostled for positions nearest to number one as possible. Songwriting teams like Goffin-King and Mann-Weil were smarting from the industry's metamorphosis inaugurated by the Beatles, and so determined were radio programmers to combat the influx of British drones, they pressured immigration authorities to curtail the amount of work permits issued to English rock stars.

Even worse, some of the biggest American pop figures were literally dying off, their obituaries personifying the end of an era: Sam Cooke was shot to death, Johnny Burnette drowned in a boating accident, and both Nat "King" Cole and pilgrim deejay Alan Freed dropped from health complications. It was extraordinarily difficult, but not impossible, for an American to have another smash hit, and Mercury believed they could repeat past success with Lesley if they could only find the ideal vessel back into the top. Just such a tune would come from a kid, a doctor, and a bad case of the flu.

# THE CHANGING OF
# THE GUARD

Trying to fight off a nasty head cold, Quincy Jones visited the office of physician Lester Coleman. With Jones unable to speak or argue with a tongue depressor stuck in his mouth, the good doctor propositioned the mogul. "Listen, I've got this godson who's written this song I think you should hear. I just know you're gonna love it!"

Jones was never closed off to ideas and readily accepted a demo from a sixteen-year-old Marvin Hamlisch, who would grow up to be one of Broadway's most productive composers. His song was the sugary confection, "Sunshine, Lollipops, and Rainbows," of which Lesley would record a jazzy version in 1963 for her *Mixed-Up Hearts* album.

But now, in the summer of '65, Lesley was scheduled to appear in another motion picture. The usual surf plot and beach blanket hijinks were transplanted to the snowy slopes, and the completed film was *Ski Party*, starring Frankie Avalon. To fill a few minutes of time in a scene involving a bus en route to a frosty ski resort, Lesley performs the perky romp for Frankie, prompting everyone else on board to sing along. At the song's conclusion, the passengers applaud, Lesley takes her seat hidden near the rear of the bus, then mysteriously disappears (did she ever get off the bus, or did they just forget her on the mountain during the return trip?).

"Sunshine, Lollipops, and Rainbows" was so sweet, it could have induced a diabetic coma, and Mercury was doubtful that the hard candy concoction could compete with the boys from the United Kingdom. Morris Diamond, who steadily promoted Gore's records, coined the slogan "Let's have Mor(e) Diamond and Les(s) Gore!" and Diamond's catchy enthusiasm, as well as his admiration for the star, seemed to warrant enough confidence from the label to release the song as a single. Decades later, Diamond still recalled his relationship with the young singer with fondness, telling radio producer Jack Roberts, "I earned the confidence of her parents, Leo and Ronny Gore, that they could entrust their daughter's activity in my hands." Having two daughters of his own, Diamond was intensely protective of the young singer, whom the promoter considered his third daughter.

And Mercury appeared to have great faith in Diamond's ability to strike the right chord with product, vendor, and venue. The record was released in June, and much to the sugar shock and delight of the label, the bubblegum symphony left a sticky trail all the way up to lucky #13. Perhaps it was the looming, terrifying prospect of being drafted into war, or perhaps it was the increasingly turbulent "youthquake" beginning to rattle social conventions, an eager audience wanted to get lost in the song's unadulterated, shameless giddiness, its joyful, almost naive celebration of young love and innocence. The song continues to enjoy the auspicious reputation of being one of the shortest to hit, clocking in at a minute and thirty-six seconds, from start to finish; the longer, original version she had recorded a couple years earlier was scrapped and replaced with the single version, set to a manic, spunkier beat to take up less film time in the movie. Lesley mused during a 2003 live concert, "It always used to make me feel funny, when these songs were selling. You used to go down to the record store and plunk down that dollar, and that dollar was hard earned each week. For some reason, whenever we sold a copy of this song, I felt compelled to return fifty cents."

Defying all expectations, the record shocked Mercury and scores of other industry insiders by being nominated for a Grammy—the singer's second nomination. Also nominated for Contemporary Rock and Roll Female Vocal Performance were Jackie DeShannon ("What the World Needs Now Is Love"), Fontella Bass ("Rescue Me"), and Barbara Lewis ("Baby, I'm Yours"), but the trophy would go to Petula Clark's equally infectious "I Know a Place."

The following month, with the song still showing action on the charts, a compilation LP was released: *The Golden Hits of Lesley*

*Gore*, sporting all of her singles, including the blissfully happy "Sunshine, Lollipops, and Rainbows." Mercury enjoyed modest sales from the album, and to keep their star firmly in the public eye, Lesley committed herself to a whirlwind of television guest spots on *Hullaballoo*, *Shindig* and *American Bandstand*, sharing the spotlight with Dionne Warwick, Martha and the Vandellas, Major Lance, and the Turtles. While continuing to meet and exceed her obligations at Sarah Lawrence (she plucked out her college essays on a typewriter that traveled with her from gig to gig), Lesley's career was flourishing in what was the peak of Lesleymania.

But the singer's steady footing would find itself on a slender ledge with Quincy Jones's sudden shift in his own personal obligations.

Jones's stature in the music community as a musician in his own right had garnered him invitations to projects outside of Mercury. After all, Jones's creativity and instincts helped turn the label from a nearly exclusive jazz outfit to a more mainstream, and profitable, pop titan. The small and silver screens came to call, and it was only natural that a man of Jones's numerous talents would be thrilled with the opportunity to exercise his gifts in different mediums, even if it meant dividing his allegiance to his roster of stars and to Lesley.

He prepared her for his leave to Hollywood, and Lesley did what she could to accommodate him, to salvage the relationship she was afraid of losing. He had begun working on the score for the 1964 Holocaust-era film, *The Pawnbroker*, starring Rod Steiger. Within two weeks, Jones was gone, living in Los Angeles to be near the motion picture epicenter. "We tried doing some sessions on the West Coast but it was wearing," Gore told Fred Bronson in 1996. "One of us had to come back and forth."

In one of their final Manhattan sessions together, Lesley recorded an original song, "My Town, My Guy, and Me." Throbbing to a bustling city beat cribbed from Petula Clark's "Downtown," a carefree Lesley proclaims she doesn't need a wild crowd or a vibrant metropolis to be happy—just her true love, her hometown, and her private niche in the world. Its flip, "A Girl in Love," is another Gore-authored tune, a driving, majestic song about a pair of shy lovers (so enamored of Gore were the Beatles that they invited her to perform the song on their 1965 television special).

"My Town, My Guy, and Me" was released in fall of 1965 and reached #32, despite poor regional play in San Francisco, one of the cities referenced within the lyric. Lesley told Dawn Eden, "We had our hands slapped for saying 'Frisco' instead of 'San Francisco.' We discovered that the people who lived in San Francisco didn't like to hear their town referred to as 'Frisco.'" As a result, radio stations in the haughty city by the bay wouldn't play the record.

Bulwarked by the successes of *Boys, Boys, Boys* and the *Golden Hits* collection, Mercury was expecting to score a hit with her fifth studio album, the very danceable *My Town, My Guy, and Me*. The LP boasted the title track, as well as a cover of "The Things We Did Last Summer," the rousing "You Don't Own Me" sound-alike "I Don't Care," and the gorgeous Wall-of-Sound "Baby That's Me" that even Phil Spector would have envied. John Lissner of WPIX-FM in New York drafted the liner notes and summed up the album by writing, "This is the first Lesley Gore album I've ever heard, and it is a revelation indeed. We 'middle-aged cats' who feed on memories of Glenn Miller and the Dorseys would do well to open our ears to worthy young talents like Lesley Gore. This young lady is the possessor of a fresh, lively, youthful, swinging sound—the dancing sound that's exciting the younger generation." The "go-go" record, as Lissner termed the complete album, is influenced by the twangy surf sound, but more so by the heavy, restless Motown beat.

Sadly, Jones's final album for his good friend barely scratched its way to #90. Mercury had to swallow two losses—the neglected album and the loss of Quincy Jones, who left the label after completing the project with Gore.

She was the darling of the '60s, the Princess of Pop, but by 1966 it was clear that Lesley Gore was losing her stronghold on the charts. Had it been just three years since her debut 45 was the top song in the United States, virtually guaranteeing hits over the next ten records? Now it seemed as if her singles were laced with poison and deejays refused to touch them, and already "It's My Party" sounded so old-fashioned and trite. Something needed to be done before Lesley Gore songs became novelties.

In the wake of Jones's vanishing, Claus Ogerman, the arranger who had created the sound of Lesley's gamut of hits, decided to take on challenging projects outside of the label as well. With the constants of her professional life suddenly and startlingly gone, Lesley was terrified of the prospect of a new producer, a new arranger, strangers who hadn't built up the history and friendship she'd gelled with Quincy and Claus. Would the new team work well together, or, better yet, would they be able to boost Lesley back into the Top 10?

Shelby Singleton took over as producer. He seemed like an odd choice; he was an A&R man for Mercury, and most of his attention was focused on country music and the baying Nashville sound. He was as uncertain of Lesley as she was of him, especially because he considered her a risk—her commitment to education was commendable, but it was like a hatchet to her music career. To save her, Singleton knew the singer needed a reinvention, a refreshed sound.

For her next album, Singleton hooked arranger Alan Lorber and Singleton's musicians from Nashville. It was an unusual cocktail, but Lorber was eager for the task of arranging for rock royalty. He wrote that Gore "was not only a great voice of pop music, but was a confident communicator of a lyric. So even though this album was the only recording we made together, it was a good marriage."

Gore was less confident, telling Fred Bronson, "It was tough for me. Shelby's a lovely man, but he was very different from Quincy. That was another lesson for me in working with other people." And the fact remained, Lesley badly missed her old friend Quincy and felt every fiber of his absence.

The first major change was Lesley's appearance. Although still conservative and preppy, her style managed to relax a little, displaying a smarter, casual attitude. And absent was the hair—the weatherproof, structurally sound flip was hacked off into a short, cropped, tightly stylized updo that reflected the look of the mid-'60s. Besides the physical makeover, Lesley was enjoying a social maturity, a political awareness that made her more than just a pop singer, more than a voice on a 45. With America embroiled in racial unrest and riots—as well as stagnating in a bloody and relentless conflict in Vietnam—Lesley was inspired to join the Democratic campaign for young, idealistic Bobby Kennedy, the enthusiastic, much-loved prince of the former White House Camelot.

Kennedy had come to Sarah Lawrence to speak on easing cultural tensions and finally bringing home exhausted servicemen from the deadly jungles overseas. Lesley told *Biography*, "Bobby Kennedy was the first person I can remember learning a social conscience from, having a desire to actually go out and help people and make this world a better place—and it was all because of him. He seemed to have so much charisma, and everything he said seemed so possible then. You looked into his eyes and I could sense that [ . . . ] he understood people's pain." Evidence of Kennedy's appeal on Gore can be traced in an interview the nineteen-year-old gave months before the senator's assassination: "I've become aware that successful show-business personalities can have a real influence on people, for good or evil. I want to be good." Not only did she diligently work for Kennedy's election campaign, but also headed the national "First Time Voters for Kennedy" to help register new voters, and sang at fundraisers, braving her fear of singing before large crowds. By 1966, entrenched in her studies and political interests, Lesley confessed to Dawn Eden that she "had done as little performing as possible, because, frankly, I was scared to death of it." At one point she began meditating and even visited a hypnotist to get her to relax more when confronted with the apprehension of live appearances. The humble and self-effacing singer inaccurately concluded in the same interview, "I didn't have the chops. It made me nervous. The studio was a safe place for me and a good learning experience, so I was comfortable in that mode."

A Gore family member confirmed the singer's anxiety to this author: "That's what people don't realize—she was scared to death.

She always appeared so calm when she performed, but she was absolutely terrified back then. She needed to be liked, but not in a vanity kind of way. She needed approval. She needed to know she still belonged."

Her development and familiarity within the recording booth was evident to Alan Lorber from the beginning. "Lesley, always business-like and prepared and without music, would walk up to the mic after one or two run-throughs, and do an almost perfect performance [ . . . ] The songs she sang, cast naturally with the right vocal range and style, had the right philosophical content for her."

The first song released from the Gore-Singleton-Lorber triad was a tune the singer composed herself with brother Michael, "I Won't Love You Anymore (Sorry)." In it, Lesley sarcastically apologizes for walking away from a romance that had been built up by a conniving, manipulative man. The verses are punctuated by small, screechy strings and a dreary, low saxophone. With a thunderous roll of timpani drums and ascending violins, the chorus lifts in a celebratory rush of swirling instruments and voices.

The music is crisp, lush, and recorded in an echo that gives it a depth and layered sound that hadn't been a part of Claus Ogerman's tightly framed arrangements. The single was a blazing example of the full-length album that was to come, but the public, who had been seeing less and less of Lesley as her last school terms consumed most of her time, could only pull the song to a disappointing #80.

The LP, *Lesley Gore Sings All About Love*, hit record stores at the end of January 1966, and the new, lavish production standards aptly represented a wiser, more grown-up singer absent of her teen idol trappings. To promote its release, Singleton quickly issued another Lesley-Michael song, "We Know We're in Love," a robust dance track where Lesley finally reveals to the folks—and anyone else who might talk down to them—that she and her partner are unquestionably devoted to each other. A confession of love to un-suspecting parents who might scoff at the young lovers, a romance kept hidden from prying eyes, friends who think it's all just a phase—these features of the lyric mark another subtle revelation into Gore's sexuality as she seems to be trying, through music, to come to terms with herself as an adult. She performed the song on the final episode of the popular *Donna Reed Show*, where she was disappointed to be portraying herself, a role that was increasingly difficult for Gore to play. Living in her own skin, she would confide later, felt harder than anything else.

The singer was further disappointed, yet again, when the single she had believed in so fervently fared only slightly better than the previous, stalling at #78.

The LP, too, sluggishly reached #66. Too many people were turning deaf ears to what was one of her finest efforts. Perhaps part of the problem were the strange song choices picked to flesh out the album; if Singleton's idea was to take an established star and revive her image, it seems incomprehensible that he would dust off moldy oldies to cover, like the Teddy Bears' 1958 classic "To Know Him Is to Love Him" and the Shirelles' "Will You Love Me Tomorrow" from 1961. Still, her renditions are some of her finest, strongest recordings, with smooth percussions, twittling flutes, and violent yet lush Wagnerian strings, all woven and braided together to create dense, rich soundscapes that would drown any other performer. Lorber's luxurious arrangements and Singleton's generous production standards enhance the singer's voice, making her vocals almost part of the orchestra itself.

In March, the album's final single would make an impression on the radio, calling deserved attention to her underappreciated new sound. Another of Singleton's remakes, this time a cover of Sonny James's "Young Love," managed to hop halfway up the charts to #50. Lorber was after a bigger sounding track than the simple, country-plucking original; though he inserted a dose of good Southwest country guitar picking as homage to the Sonny James original, this new version would become an updraft of breezy strings and a deeply wailing soprano sax, all saturated in an expansive, canyonlike echo chamber.

The public responded warmly to the record, turning it into a sizable success. An audience was still there for Lesley Gore tunes,

"Young Love" confirmed. She appeared on *Hullaballoo* to promote the song; the receptive, cheering crowd that drowned out the first strains of her performance and silenced the end of it, gave her the emotional boost she sorely needed, an injection of confidence that assuaged some of the heartache over her recent run of chart failures. The fans were still listening. The career still had vitality in it.

What Lesley had no way of knowing while still basking in the limelight of another hit single was that "Young Love" would be her last chart entry for almost an entire year, which in "industry time" is enough to bury a career.

# CALIFORNIA DREAMING

Lesley was anxious to put out another record and keep the momentum whizzing. Songwriters Carole Bayer and Toni Wine had just put the finishing touches on their latest song, and before the ink could dry on the sheet music, Lesley dragged the women and their composition to Shelby Singleton.

"I love this song," Lesley said resolutely as the producer scanned the lyrics. "This is the one I want to do."

"'A Groovy Kind of Love,'" Singleton muttered, mulling it over. "Change the word 'groovy.'"

Carole looked as if she'd been slammed in the stomach with a battering ram. "What?"

"Take out 'groovy,'" the producer repeated. "It's too slangy, too corny."

Carole's eyes instantly glistened with tears. Lesley consoled her later, "Leave it in. Don't you change a single word. I think it's a great song."

Singleton refused to record Carole's song. Instead, it was handed over to the Mindbenders, a British group on a Mercury subsidiary, and they took "A Groovy Kind of Love" to #2. It could have been the hit Gore needed to reclaim the pop charts, and the Mindbenders' tremendous success did not go unnoticed by a remorseful Lesley. "It would have been a really good record for me," she lamented decades later.

Frustrated by the loss of "Groovy Kind of Love," Lesley made the trek to Los Angeles to record a few sides with her painfully missed friend and mentor, Quincy Jones. At home with him in his West Coast studio, the pair recorded half a dozen tracks for a potential new full-length album. One of them, another Bayer-Wine piece, became the first single to hit the radio. "Off and Running," a boisterous rocker replete with hand claps, maracas, and a raunchy surf guitar, was released in June 1966 just at the start of the halcyon days of summer. It was a perfect beach song, debuting at the height of the surf cycle, and Lesley's obvious affection for the material shines through every rowdy beat. "Off and Running," however, would trip and fall at the starting line, not even close to breaking into the Top 100.

Jones had given Lesley his best effort musically as usual; but the song was given no promotion, and the producer was too engrossed in larger, costlier ventures in his California outfit to devote much time and attention to Lesley, so the singer begrudgingly skulked back to New York to face her fading success—and another new producer.

Bob Crewe had been waiting a long time to get his hands on Lesley Gore. Born in New Jersey in 1937, Crewe grew up to be a talented songwriter, arranger, and producer, joining the ranks of great ones like Quincy Jones and Phil Spector. He first enjoyed success in 1957 when he produced the Rays' immortal "Silhouettes," and continued to rack up hit records supporting acts like the Diamonds and Freddy "Boom Boom" Cannon. In the early '60s, his songwriting talents would launch Frankie Valli and the Four Seasons into orbit with their classic string of hits "Sherry," "Big Girls Don't Cry," "Walk Like a Man," and "Ragdoll." It didn't hurt that he was also tall, blond, and handsome, making his own hit record, "Music to Watch Girls By," a simple sell.

Crewe was a force to be reckoned with, so when he first heard "It's My Party," he began to sift through the pink, perfumed copy-cats that followed in Gore's wake, looking for the right girl to groom to emulate Lesley's persona and success. His first attempt was with Tracey Dey, whose cute, clever songs couldn't break into the Top 50. His next acquisition was Diane Renay, whose uncanny similarity to Gore in voice and appearance gave Crewe an edge into the market. Taking a cue from the Shirelles' "Soldier Boy" and Jamie Horton's "My Little Marine," Diane Renay's hit record, "Navy Blue," docked ship at #6. But Crewe was never able to recapture the charm or popularity of Diane Renay's only hit, and she became another victim of the girl-group extinction.

Now, in 1966, Crewe was thrilled to have the real thing, and he immediately set out to salvage Lesley's quickly decaying career. His first offering was his "Treat Me Like a Lady," an unusual fusion of pure white pop with the horse-clomping Motown beat of the Supremes' "Baby Love." The creative and lovely record was a dismal failure.

Undaunted, Crewe found for her an eerie miniature symphony composed of several unique parts and sounds, another contribution from songwriter Marvin Hamlisch. Borrowing the crisp style of pop and an exuberant swing from traditional jazz, "California Nights" celebrated the warmth and romantic glorification of the Golden Coast and the dreamy enigma of Southern California. Lesley was drawn to the song and its arrangement, smitten with the visuals Crewe was able to paint with notes, chords, and rhythms.

The verses pulse to a lonely bass guitar, a haunting and faraway clarinet, shy handclaps that keep a lazy tempo, all playing over the soft, misty sound of waves caressing the shoreline. Like saltwater breaking on the sand, the chorus crescendos in a cymbal-crashing, violin-saturated frenzy of sun worship, undulating to another of Crewe's imaginative, inimitable drum lines.

The sensual lyrics and three-dimensional arrangement created a musical portrait. Released in chilly January 1967, "California Nights" evoked the anticipation and longing for warmer weather, and fans loved the touch of suntan lotion in winter. The song basked in the chartshine at #16, revitalizing Lesley's stature on the scene.

Promoting the song led Lesley to make the usual rounds of television, with one particular appearance a marked difference from the rest. *Batman*, the surprising monster hit and guilty pleasure that starred Adam West as a paunchy caped crusader (and a bevy of big-name celebrities as the colorful parade of villains bringing chaos to Gotham City), invited Lesley to sing "California Nights" on the show. An implausible plotline (worked into yet another of the series' implausible plotlines) introduced the singer in pink tights and fuzzy ears as "Pink Pussycat," the henchwoman to the fierce

Catwoman, played by the indomitable, ageless Julie Newmar. Pink Pussycat, harboring a crush on the Boy Wonder, also lilts "Maybe Now," a cut from her newest album; "I'm not the type of girl to kiss a boy on the first crime," she coos to a ferociously randy Robin. Gore joked during a 2006 concert, "I still have that costume hanging in my closet."

Thanks to Crewe, Lesley found her career on a severely needed upswing. The only thing more surprising than "Sunshine, Lollipops, and Rainbows" being nominated for a Grammy was that the eloquent and musically superior "California Nights" was blatantly overlooked, though competition that year was crowded with worthy candidates (Aretha Franklin, Petula Clark, and the sultry Bobbie Gentry, with her enigmatic "Ode to Billie Joe," swept the ceremony). Beyond Lesley's musical success in early 1967, she enjoyed a stint that summer in her first stage play at the Valley Forge Music Fair, *Half a Sixpence*, starring Tony Tanner.

Her renewed popularity brought legions of new fans along with the following growing up beside her from "It's My Party" days. But the increase in TV spots and radio play brought her the unwanted, terrifying attention of one loyal, obsessive fan.

It began with menacing letters—pages and pages of hand-scrawled rants and threats poured from the deranged mind of a dangerous man. The stalker wrote frequently, and when letters didn't bring him as close to her as he wanted, he discovered a way to speak to her personally.

She felt almost outside of herself, like watching the beleaguered heroine in a horror movie. The stalker began with incessant phone calls to the school, lying to school administrators and manipulating them into putting her on the line with him. He pursued her this way for months, until one phone call came in that announced he was coming across the country to get her.

With no way to trace where the attacker was, Lesley stayed holed up at school or at home, thirty minutes away. She kept a close watch over her shoulder when she had to be in public places.

Early publicity still of the newly crowned "Princess of Pop." (Michael Ochs Archives/Getty Images)

Alone in the spotlight, the diminutive Lesley Gore was a surprising female powerhouse of the 1960s. (ABC/Photofest)

A nervous Gore appears with Ed Sullivan on the granddaddy of all TV variety shows. (Photofest)

The Gore family celebrates in 1964; from left to right, Michael, Leo, Lesley, and Ronny. (David Magnus/Rex USA)

Gore on the set of *Hullaballoo* with Trini Lopez and Dionne Warwick. (Michael Ochs Archives/Getty Images)

Gore's legendary appearance on *The TAMI Show* filmed concert. (Michael Ochs Archives/Getty Images)

Gore shut down production of the surf-and-turf romp *Girls on the Beach* when she contracted a contagious case of the measles. (Everett Collection)

Gore performs "Sunshine, Lollipops, and Rainbows" in the film *Ski Party*. (Everett Collection)

Then, as the nightmare played itself out, the man who'd threatened to catch her arrived on the campus of Sarah Lawrence. Gore was tipped off by a friend to stay out of sight, and when her pursuer couldn't find her, his rage became physical. He stormed into the cafeteria and scanned the frightened faces of the young ladies, demanding to know where he could find his target. When no one helped, the man flew into a violent fury and turned over tables and launched chairs at the walls.

Lesley stayed hidden as police rushed the university. They subdued the sociopath and swiftly sent him back home—and to jail. Although Lesley breathed a sigh of relief and returned to classes, her troubles were not yet over.

By May 1967, Lesley realized that the success of "California Nights" was only temporary. The single had long since dropped off the charts and was replaced by another Crewe musical mural, "Summer and Sandy." A miniature symphony constructed in three parts, "Sandy" is another tribute to the beach and hot dog season that Crewe helped compose to cash in on the success of "California Nights." The verses mimic the same happy swing, complete with the weaving of sound effects (this time, it's the whisper of a cool, salty sea breeze). In the background, quivering strings echo the haunting melody of "A Summer Place"—typical of Crewe's unique flourishes and ear for detail. Next, the chorus launches into eerie minor chords over a driving, rapid-fire drum track. Finally, as the song fades to an end, Lesley quietly adlibs above the deep, slow Ronettes-style timpani beats.

Like its predecessor, "Summer and Sandy" was a triumph artistically, but its poor public reception at #65 proved "Summer and Sandy" was musical seaweed. It appeared on the full-length album *California Nights*, released that summer to sales only modest enough to drag the LP into the Top 100 at #69. The songs Crewe handpicked for the album exhibited the range of Lesley's voice—the even, sultry lows on "Lilacs and Violets"; the soaring, pitch-perfect highs of "I'm Going Out (The Same Way I Came In)"; fierce melodramas like "Bad" and the brassy "The Bubble Broke"; a sooth-ing Jackie DeShannon style waltz, "Love Goes On Forever"; and the album was rounded out with a Lesley-Michael tune, "Maybe Now."

Crewe had given Lesley both a hit and a miss, and was eager to start a new project with the singer. Unfortunately, Mercury felt the one hit was not enough and the one flop was too much, so they yanked their star away from the best collaborator she'd had since Quincy Jones and handed her over to producer Steve Douglas, who had different ideas for the former Princess of Pop and yet another reinvention of her image.

Nineteen sixty-seven marked the threshold of the Summer of Love—uninhibited sex, experimentation with hallucinatory drugs, and a rejection of violence and 1950s Victorian sensibilities. Young people across America grew distrustful of the government and furious with the devastating, staggering death toll in 1967 alone of 6,000 US troops, and another 30,000 wounded, in what was increasingly being viewed as a senseless war in Vietnam. At home, race riots in impoverished cities burned as people of color fell victim to blatant police brutality and simmering economic inequities. Even mom and dad—those enemies over thirty sharing the dinner table—were considered part of the Establishment whom the Flower Children felt were leading the country into social ruin.

Floundering in the destruction wrought by the British Invasion, then by the Cultural Revolution, rockers from the '50s and early '60s found few options for their particular brands. Some deserted rock and crossed the Rio Grande into country-and-western music; Brenda Lee, Conway Twitty, Sue Thompson, and Dickie Lee would all enjoy another decade of success plucking guitar strings and steel guitars. Others simply disappeared altogether, like Connie Francis, who, reeling from an emotionally traumatizing sexual assault in her motel room following a live performance, left the recording studio and found her career hopelessly out of sync with the tastes of modern America, with her own mental wellness on the brink. A few artists bravely ventured into the new frontier, but the Murmaids could find no takers with their cover of Traffic's "Paper Sun," and when the Chiffons released "Nobody Knows What's Going On in My Mind But Me," Irwin Chusid of WFMU, New Jersey, glibly noted, "Nobody seemed to care."

The girl-group sound, of which Lesley was a purveyor, took only seven fast years to sprout, blossom, peak, and wither away to mulch. By the summer of 1967, top records belonged to the ferocious Jefferson Airplane ("Somebody to Love"), psychedelic rock bands like Strawberry Alarm Clock ("Incense & Peppermints"), flower children like Scott McKenzie ("San Francisco"), and acid-tripping hits from the Beatles ("Strawberry Fields Forever" and "All You Need Is Love"). These were the new stars of AM radio—garage bands and hippies, anti-violence punk groups and pro-peace folk singers. The idealized days of the postwar American Dream were dead, buried, and decomposing. This new generation did not want to look or act like their conservative parents, and young people were searching for idols that represented them and their anger at Big Brother.

Lesley Gore was a big square.

Producer Steve Douglas had his own personal stake in girl groups—he'd been the fantastic lead saxophonist on several Crystals and Ronettes records, and a producer on many hits pumped out of the Gold Star Studios in the early '60s. He followed musical fads and discovered and promoted psychedelic bands, solidifying his foothold in music well into the end of the decade. Considering his role in Phil Spector's miniature epics and his probing of mysterious sonic landscapes, Douglas was optimistic and excited to be teamed with Gore, who was seeking a new direction herself; she wanted to stay in the rock arena, to apply her talent to changing tastes rather than be put out to pasture like too many of her radio contemporaries. After all, some pop acts had successfully transitioned with the radical shifts and had musical muscle left to flex, like Bobby Vee with his groovy "Come Back When You Grow Up" and the Shangri-Las' powerful, chilling depiction of a rape victim healing from her attack in "Past, Present, and Future."

The Los Angeles–based producer brought Lesley to California to be near the cultural decadence sprung from Haight-Asbury and Golden Gate Park, in an attempt to inject Lesley into the West Coast mindwarp market that was raging and massive. Setting up house in the famed Beverly Hills Hotel (already a tony move that ran counter to what Gore and Douglas were trying to fabricate), Lesley reported for work on August 15, 1967, at United Recorders, 6050 Sunset Boulevard.

By the end of their first session, the pair completed both sides of their premier 45. The superb A-side was "Brink of Disaster," one of her best singles of the '60s. Set to a big Beach Boys backbeat with a Spector-esque wall of sound, the song begins with her conscience (implied by her deadpan voice filtered through a tinny megaphone) warning the ill-fated singer that her blind infatuation will only get her into trouble. Her double-tracked voice responds with her thick-headed decision to pursue the noncommittal boy, even though she clearly knows she ought to avoid him. He's a repeat offender, she's played the game before, and the emotional heart betters the logical head in the end.

The flip is another cheerful tune, "On a Day Like Today," where the narrator wastes no time in hooking up with the guy who lives down the hall after her boyfriend packs up and leaves her apartment.

Critics loved the release, complimenting the catchy melodies and clever constructions of both sides. Heavy play in Los Angeles, San Francisco, and New York brought positive vibes of good things to come. But within a month after its debut, the prophetically titled "Brink of Disaster" hardly brushed the Top 100 at #82 and, unbeknownst to anyone at the time, would mark her final appearance on the American pop charts.

"Brink of Disaster" seemed to foretell the swift and sad decline of Lesley Gore's remarkable career with Mercury. As Douglas continued to compile tracks for her next studio album, Mercury released Gore's next single, "Magic Colors," which blended rich Beach Boy harmonies with a heavy, dreamy psychedelia. The song came from writing gurus Neil Sedaka and Howard Greenfield, whose combined talents were responsible for Sedaka's unstoppable train of monster hits in the first half of the decade. Having helmed the popular "Little Sister," Coca-Cola radio jingles Lesley recorded in the mid-'60s, Sedaka and Greenfield contributed "Magic Colors" as the essential song on the LP of the same name; "I was thrilled when she recorded my song," Sedaka told this author. A downbeat, grim entry, a lost love has left Lesley's world a tattered and whitewashed wasteland, and the singer wonders what has become of all the magic colors that used to paint her life. The B-side was a bouncy cover of the Tokens' "It's a Happening World"; but the public didn't care for either of Lesley's worlds, and Mercury saw the writing on the wall.

The LP *Magic Colors* was slated for a Christmas release, and Lesley was hoping the singles would have at least generated a little interest among listeners to give the complete album a try. Where Shelby Singleton tried connecting the songs on *All About Love* through lavish, pulsing arrangements, Steve Douglas wanted *Magic Colors* to be a coherent, morose experiment in mood, woven together by inventive, dreamlike tracks with a soupcon of medieval minstrel darkness.

Besides the two singles and their flipsides, the album contains the ballad "You Sent Me Silver Bells," about a soldier returning home in a casket from the Vietnamese battlegrounds. There is the rousing "I'm Fallin' Down," and the slow and smooth "He Won't See the Light," blending a harpsichord with fluttery guitars for a Spanish flavor. Lesley and her brother contributed "Where Can I Go," and the album is completed by a pair of lovely but mostly needless carbon-copy remakes of "To Sir with Love" and "How Can I Be Sure," which occupy space on the album that might have been better served with original material.

*Magic Colors* was certainly a drastic departure in theme and content from Gore's usual output, and Douglas believed in his vision despite the dismal sales of the two singles. He was confident that the unique and densely detailed collection would make an impact on the drug-induced buying audience and garner legions of new fans disenchanted by the conservative status quo.

Executives at Mercury didn't quite see things through the same hazy glasses. For starters, the ambitious intentions and novelty of *Magic Colors* were not a match for Lesley Gore, who did not do drugs, who was not a flower child, and who was a mainstream pop singer; this new makeover was simply too difficult to believe, to promote, and to sell. Modern songs listed toward political, literary lyrics, while *Magic Colors*, for all its lava lamp and tie-dyed posturing, couldn't hide the fact that the songs were still Gore's standard sad love songs disguised in beads and hippie dregs. Besides the almost comical mismatch of music and persona, Mercury analyzed the current singles sales and projected the marketability of this new album; speaking in dollars, the label had only dire predictions.

Gore and Douglas were crushed to learn that Mercury's final decision was to shelve *Magic Colors*. What would have been the singer's eighth complete album was archived and wouldn't be made public for nearly thirty years.

Lesley Gore had been one of Mercury's hottest acts, sometimes outselling records by those of her labelmates. To show their appreciation, the label was sweeping her latest project into the vaults. After five years, it appeared that the singer and her handlers were tiring of each other.

She had still one year left to fulfill on her contract, and Mercury seemed only to pass the time until the terms of the contract lapsed. Nineteen sixty-eight began with Lesley being bounced from producer to producer in a last ditch effort to secure a hit. Though she recorded decent but unspectacular songs, the feverish pace and rapid output of material couldn't generate enough heat to light a match, and the jockeying for serviceable compositions seemed to reveal a quiet but growing desperation.

First, Charles Koppelman and Don Robin brought Lesley into the studio and pumped out five sides. The first three—"Sleep Tight," "I'm with You," and "Me About You"—were either lost or unissued. Two songs survived and were quickly released in February 1968. The A-side "Small Talk," was a playful, breezy, echo-saturated pure pop track. Its flip, "Say What You See," was the stronger, horn-laden, Association-influenced song. The record, with songs from either side competing for attention, came and went in a matter of weeks and no one seemed to notice.

Next, Herb Bernstein snagged "He Gives Me Love (La La La)" from the Eurovision Song Contest, which would later plop ABBA onto international turntables. Originally recorded by Spanish singer Massiel, Lesley's cover of "He Gives Me Love" was a solidly delivered rendition, retaining the feel and tone of traditional Spanish folk music, with an extra Mediterranean frill also heard in Gene Pitney's "True Love Never Runs Smooth" and Petula Clark's "This Is My Song." Again, the single was released and flopped (although it did crawl into the nineties on the Easy Listening chart).

The fluffy love songs were pulling Lesley even further out to sea. Listeners preferred the grits of Dusty Springfield, or the concrete and gravel voice of salt-of-the-earth, tragic Janis Joplin.

Across the globe, guerilla newsmen filmed images that brought American viewers closer to war than ever before, as television screens flickered with the images of gun battles, executions, and young soldiers dragged lifelessly through swamps as their terrified comrades scrambled for safety. Protestors burned their draft cards, and even stalwart conservatives were disgusted by the cruel and dehumanizing massacre at My Lai, where infantry troops were commanded to raid the tiny village and destroy it to its foundations. In under half an hour, 450 innocent men, women, and children were sprayed with bullets and burned alive in their homes. The only survivors were "those who had been buried under the bodies of the dead," according to one report.

Back on US soil, the shocking assassination of peaceful civil rights leader Martin Luther King Jr. left cities burning in the wake of coast-to-coast rioting. King had landed in Memphis, Tennessee, to defend city sanitation employees striking for better work benefits. "It really doesn't matter what happens now," King said upon his arrival. "I've been to the mountaintop [ . . . ] so I'm happy tonight. I'm not fearing any man." The next evening, April 4, King appeared on the balcony of his Lorraine Motel room. A rifle blast from across the street tore into King's throat, "penetrating his spinal cord and hurling him back against the wall," according to witness testimony. King's companions tried to stabilize the gaping wound, but their best efforts could not save the modern pilgrim of human civil rights.

The deepest cut for Lesley would come a couple of months later as she was watching TV in her dorm room on the night of June 4. In the ballroom of the Ambassador Hotel in Los Angeles, young, enthusiastic Robert F. Kennedy had just proven victorious in the California presidential primary. "My thanks to all of you," the grinning candidate proclaimed to the cameras, "and now it's on to Chicago, and let's win there!" Then, just moments later, he was sprawled out on the floor of the hotel kitchen, bleeding profusely from a gunshot to his neck. Before that night was over, Kennedy was gone, taking with him the prospect of another Camelot and the promise of a gentler, more socially progressive America.

Lesley was crushed by the loss of her admired political hero. She jumped on the line with her press agent, who had immediate and closer access to the situation, and the weeping friends consoled one another over a twelve-hour phone call. Compounding her grief and her personal sympathies with young protestors seeking policy and civil changes, the singer still worked at preserving Mercury's finely-groomed baby-shampoo image of Lesley Gore: When asked by a Pittsburgh newspaper for her thoughts about the civil unrests flaring up across US college campuses, the docile singer replied with a safe, virtuous, "When students take the responsibility of breaking the law, they must take the consequences."

Almost as a response to the death of her great, lost leader, Lesley's next single in August 1968 was the Bernstein-produced, "I Can't Make It Without You." One of her most somber entries, the despairing song depicts endless days weeping, a life not worth living, happy treasures that have become instruments of emotional torture, a world filled with beautiful things suddenly turned ugly—all over the loss of love, the loss of something great. Horns blast the frightening three-note introduction of Bach's "Toccata and Fugues in D-Minor," and the song dissolves into a quiet, funereal harp and haunting woodwind. "I Can't Make It Without You" acutely reflected the tumultuous summer of 1968 that saw the expulsion of three US Olympic athletes for their "black power" salute, rioting in Chicago in response to the unpopular selection of Hubert Humphrey as Democratic nominee for the office of the presidency, and the incomprehensible number of US soldiers killed in the war—now surpassing 30,000. The song was viscerally striking and the best single to come out of the hodgepodge of revolving door producers. This dose of hurt and melancholia seemed destined to hit big—but again, the song was a bomb, coming and going as if it had never existed and veering away from the Top 100.

Lesley couldn't give away her records. She had to do something—*anything*—to distract herself from her plummeting fame and eroding career.

# LAST CALL

With an all-too-long chain of chart catastrophes, and wary of the chaos in California, an exasperated Lesley fled to the East Coast and turned to another venue in which to aim her expanding talents: acting.

She had already made a few cheesy cameos in surf movies and TV's *Batman*, but got to experience playing someone other than herself with her role in the previous year's *Half a Sixpence*. In 1968, she performed in two nationally touring summer-stock productions. She first starred in *Funny Girl*, and the *Spring Herald* recognized that the play "leans heavily on the talents of the actress in the title role. In this respect, the current production is fortunate to have Lesley Gore. Her rendition of 'People' came close to stopping the performance, and she was never more winsome and tender in the lovely ballad, 'Who Are You Now?'"

Similarly glowing reviews followed for her role in *Finian's Rainbow*. Writer Terry Kay of the *Atlantic Journal* praised, "Vocally there should be little doubt that Miss Gore is capable of excelling before an audience, but there is more, much more to her performance as Sharon. She turns nuances into lovely moments of personality and she stimulates each scene she's in." Lesley was finding comfort in living in someone else's shoes, creating a three-dimensional life spun from fiction when her own real life—with a professional career in decline and a repressed sexuality not allowing for a personal relationship—was getting harder to bear.

Lesley's first true love was making music—after all, her name was synonymous with it, and she wasn't known for anything else. Her final spate of producers, Philadelphia-grown Kenny Gamble and Leon Huff, attempted to redesign the singer's sound. Their first release was the peppy "I'll Be Standing By," a Motown track better suited for the Jackson Five. Lesley's voice is strong and capable, but not enough to salvage the problematic material. "It wasn't the best stuff for me," Gore would admit years later at a 2006 live event, "but we sure tried like hell."

To try to supplement her strange new "blue-eyed soul" single, Mercury issued a compilation album, *Lesley Gore Golden Hits Volume 2*, spanning her music following "My Town, My Guy, and Me." The collection sank, taking "I'll Be Standing By" down with it. The single was the third "reinvention" of Lesley Gore in just two years, and the general public didn't take to the latest incarnation of the singer, either.

Nineteen sixty-eight was also the year that Lesley graduated from Sarah Lawrence with a Bachelor of Arts in English. Leo and Ronny were immensely proud of their daughter, who had already experienced more life than many people do in an entire existence.

Still, at twenty-two years old and fresh out of college, Lesley was in the odd position of trying to resuscitate a career in shambles while her fellow graduates were on the cusp of beginning theirs. The musical scene—as well as the industry itself—had transformed while she was studying for exams and typing essays for literature courses, and this damaged her recording career more than any other factor, this inability to stay current, to stay vital. She was flanked on either side by opposing styles of music—soulful Motown, which was one of the few genres that survived the British Invasion, and acid-drenched rock—and neither provided her an easy segue into public acceptance.

Michael watched his sister struggle in this new climate, telling *Biography*, "It was very hard to go from having number one songs on the radio to being replaced by other artists."

Songwriter Ellie Greenwich agreed that Gore's passion and talent for music compelled the singer to keep burrowing back into the industry to reclaim a place for herself.

Even more frustrating than the career she couldn't revive was the exclusive method by which Gamble and Huff produced their records. Quincy Jones had worked tightly with his star, tutoring her on mechanics and techniques, and giving her perspective and opinions serious consideration. But the Philly duo kept Lesley at arm's length, except when they required her voice. Alfred Hitchcock famously called actors "cattle," considering them attractive props to achieve his overall aesthetic goal—the perfect visual composition, a study in angles and light and shadow. Gamble and Huff worked in much the same way, designing first a dynamite backing track and filling in the space later with a singer—any singer. "They sent me material and if I liked the song, they built a track and I just showed up and they'd point to me. I thought they made good records, but that wasn't the way I conceived of making records for myself, without any input," Lesley told Fred Bronson.

Their next single together was another funk tirade, "Take Good Care (Of My Heart)." Again, Lesley's earnest performance saves the stray Motown record that just doesn't seem to fit or enhance her voice, losing her in the overproduction of the arrangement. With the final months of her contract under Mercury winding down, commercial expediency was certainly the reason for the failure of producers and singer to develop together a smarter, cohesive style that may have rescued Lesley's floundering career. The February 1969 release of "Take Good Care" was an even bigger failure, and nothing more was to come of the fruitless Gore-Gamble-Huff combination.

To counter her scarce record sales, Lesley turned to the medium that would reach the widest mass of people and fans: the living room television set.

Since graduating college and having nothing but time, she earned roles in a couple more theater productions (*South Pacific* and *There's a Girl in My Soup*, opposite Bill Bixby) and made the rounds on an eclectic sampling of popular TV programs. Twice she dropped by *The Joey Bishop Show* to gab with the rat packer. She also stopped for a visit at Hugh Hefner's place on his swinging variety show, *Playboy After Dark*. After having to tolerate a couple of lame, horribly unfunny comedy skits with Hef and his bunnies, she finally got to sing. Backed by piano and bongo, Lesley waxed a jazzy cover of "Young Lovers" and delivered a sad, remarkable rendition of "Didn't We." With her sleek "bullet" haircut sharpening her facial features, she looks stronger, more mature and adult, and her performance is assured and confident.

Capping off her TV appearances for the year was a guest spot on a music special for ABC where she performed a lily-white but nevertheless charming version of Aretha Franklin's "Natural Woman," followed by a guest appearance (alongside the Muppets!) on Soupy Sales's kiddie show, *The Pied Piper of Astroworld*. Sales, in green tights and brandishing a magical flute, leads children through a magical fantasyland (actually, it was a Z-grade theme park in Houston, Texas). Floating down a waterway in a giant teacup, Lesley sings the mellow "Feeling Groovy." Later in the broadcast, sitting among children, farm animals, and puppets, she performs "If We Could Talk to the Animals." Throughout her guest appearance, she managed to keep her poise and a straight face.

Even corny publicity was better than none, so she humbly accepted the mediocre TV spots while she continued her uphill battle in the studio for a chart hit and a little attention. Working now with producer Paul Leka, who showed a greater appreciation for the singer, she recorded "98.6/Lazy Day," a cheerful little song ideal for its May release date. Its flip, the Sedaka-Greenfield "Summer Symphony," is a shimmering, string-saturated celebration of the season. The detailed, multilayered tracks on both sides snagged a #36 spot on the Easy Listening chart, but nationally the single was just a whimsical afterthought.

Again, Leka supervised her next session, a rendition of Laura Nyro's "Wedding Bell Blues." Lesley had been a longtime fan of the sad-eyed songwriter's trendsetting style, a fusion of contemporary pop with a suggestion of jazz; Nyro would be responsible for massive hits like "Eli's Coming" for the Three Dog Night and "Stoney End" for Barbara Streisand, before Nyro's untimely death at 49 from ovarian cancer. Trade magazines proffered early praise for Lesley's take on "Wedding Bell Blues," and Mercury held its breath in anticipation of a hit as the single began its ascension up the charts, and a fresh start for the decade for Gore.

Unknown to anyone at Mercury, the vocal group, Fifth Dimension, recorded their own version of Nyro's song. Coming off the astronomical success of "Aquarius/Let the Sunshine In," the group walked "Wedding Bell Blues" straight down the aisle to #1; Lesley's single was the forgotten bridesmaid, bawling off to the side.

By the conclusion of 1969, Lesley's contract with Mercury was at its end, forcing the singer and her label to face some weighty decisions. The former needed to decide if she should stay or go, the latter unsure if they wanted to renew or release.

Lesley had remained friends with Bob Crewe, the producer of "California Nights," who had grown disgusted with the restrictions and limitations of giant labels and struck out on his own to establish his New York–based Crewe Records. After Mercury denied him the opportunity to work with the singer again, he kept a close watch on her valiant efforts that kept hitting rock bottom. He tried to sway her over to his operation, but Lesley was uneasy about leaving the security of the only label she'd ever known, the label that had racked up hit after hit for her since her virginal record, "It's My Party." She grew up in the studios there, her records displaying her progression from teenager to independent young adult. She reasoned that it was only a matter of time before the right song came along at just the right time; after all, they'd been so close with "Wedding Bell Blues." No, she decided, I'm safe where I am. She resolved to stay.

But Mercury wasn't as optimistic about their relationship with Gore. They had run her through a series of producers on the payroll—some better and more creative than others—and still couldn't generate another hit. They also allowed the singer to sample a musical buffet of genres to try to find one that hit the spot—rock, rhythm and blues, Motown, jazz, and soul. The production costs of Gore's increasingly lavish, expansive recordings were not cheap. The common denominator, then, through Mercury's eyes, had to have been Lesley Gore, who had lost her appeal among listeners during the industry's dramatic evolution. Executives believed, despite their best efforts to save her, Lesley was a relic of a different time.

So how did they reward the star who had been their flagship into the bustling new teen market? How did they show gratitude to the singer whose voice made her bosses very wealthy men? According to the label's accounting department, the singer had accumulated a substantial debt in the amount of $175,000 from production and touring costs, leaving them no choice, they claimed, but to withhold earnings, and after seven bountiful years, Mercury Records dropped Lesley Gore from her contract.

Her career, for all outward appearances, was over.

Part Two

# SOMEPLACE ELSE NOW

# WHEN YESTERDAY WAS TOMORROW

Lesley Gore's "lost years," when the '60s rolled over into the '70s, were anything but that. Struggling to find her footing (and another hit record), she was actively recording what became some of the most luminous, complex, and confounding singles of her career. Gore fiercely asserted, "I didn't disappear."

Her final two years with Mercury might be most remembered for their near hits and misses—a potentially lucrative full-length album was not issued, and two singles that could have saved her career were instead propelled into rock history by the Mindbenders and the Fifth Dimension. And with old friends like Quincy Jones, Claus Ogerman, and Phil Ramone gone, there were no familiar faces to tell her good-bye or wish her luck as she moved into a frighteningly uncertain future.

Bob Crewe's earlier offer to join him resonated with Lesley, and she reunited with the producer in hopes of musical CPR and public TLC. Crewe was ecstatic about having Lesley join his list of talent. Having worked wonders for Frankie Valli and Diane Renay, he was glad to have an established name on his fledgling label. Since Gore wasn't some undiscovered ingénue in need of grooming and training, his challenge was not to create a new star, but to reignite a dormant one.

The seven existing sides Lesley recorded for Crewe in 1970 remain some of the best, most intriguing songs in the Gore canon. The first single, rushed to release in January, was "Why Doesn't Love Make Me Happy." The tune about a painful romance moves along to a gentle, pattering drum line, reinforced by muted, synthesized strings. Lesley is not overdubbed, thereby shedding her former "girl group" confines; instead, her voice is tender and yielding, and she allows her voice to cry out over the otherwise gentle ballad during its bitter bridges. "Why Doesn't Love Make Me Happy" was a splendid beginning for the pair—the song is a subtle tribute to Crewe's genius with sound and composition, and a shining showcase for Lesley's controlled yet emotional performance.

The record's B-side, perhaps the weakest of the Crewe recordings only in comparison to the others, was "Tomorrow's Children." Like Elvis Presley's "In the Ghetto" and Joanie Sommers's "The Great Divide," "Children" is Gore's contribution to that subgenre of music that trumpets social issues and civic responsibility, and is unique for being the only of all of Gore's recordings to comment directly on the times. Backed (and sometimes overpowered) by backing vocals that sound like the Mamas and the Papas, the song rhetorically asks modern youth, "Are we so lost / Have we no chance of finding our way" in a world overrun by violence, indifference, and intoler-ance, and answers itself by proclaiming that this new generation—tomorrow's children—can alter the future to one of love and understanding. Lesley gives a spirited performance that's half *Hair*, half public service announcement.

"Why Doesn't Love Make Me Happy" garnered favorable reviews by those who paid attention, and Crewe was rewarded with a #39 record on the Easy Listening chart. There was hope after all, so Crewe took his time—nearly four months—selecting, then fine-tuning the next single.

He decided to take advantage of the renewed popularity of duets (thanks to Sonny and Cher and Marvin Gaye and Tammy Tyrell). For the male half of the duo, Crewe selected singer Oliver, who had enjoyed success under Crewe with the release of "Good Morning Starshine" in 1969. Oliver and Lesley were billed under the aliases "Billy and Sue" (Crewe thought the instant connection to the charac-ters in the hugely successful play *Hair* would touch younger, hipper listeners), and together they recorded a groovy remake of the Fleet-woods' 1959 lullaby, "Come Softly to Me." Like he did with "Summer and Sandy," Crewe wanted to piece the track together as a series of separate movements, effectively creating a majestic, broad sound out of a simple three-chord melody.

After a dreamy, psychedelic mesh of background singers introduces the bare chord changes, Oliver begins the familiar "Mm-dooby-do-dom-dom," as Lesley, in a low and sultry tone, breathes the verse over a plucky beat filled out with rattling tambourines, Spanish guitar riffs, and clomping tom-toms and bongos. For a few bars, the instruments pause for the pair to sing and harmonize to themselves a capella, then, as the key shifts higher and higher, the backing track crashes into a relentless dance beat. Oliver's plaintive voice croons over Lesley's double-tracked, deeper register that seems to fill the background of the entire track like a canvas upon which the rest of the song is painted.

The record's flipside was an instrumental version of the song, so as not to detract from the powerful commercial side. Released in May with brimming optimism (*Billboard* had predicted a "left field summertime smash"), Billy and Sue's "Come Softly to Me" vanished almost as soon as it had arrived. The failure of the outstanding single was disheartening to Crewe; the public was ignoring his miniature masterpieces and underappreciating the flawless performances of his singer. With each release he thought he'd found the perfect vehicle to catapult Lesley back into her former stature. Even worse, the records weren't returning the profit he needed to keep his new label alive.

Taking a hint from Mary Hopkin's smash "Those Were the Days," Crewe pieced together Lesley's next unusual release, "When Yesterday Was Tomorrow." The Romani-style tune, told in minor keys and slapped tambourines that conjure up the image of moonlit, fog-enshrouded gypsy caravans, concerns a lost love and remorse. Two versions were recorded—the shorter radio edit and the longer version that included Gore's haunting chanting in languages as diverse as French, German, and Hebrew.

On the single's more attractive B-side, "Why Me, Why You," Lesley harmonizes and echoes herself as she ponders the sense of remaining in an on-and-off-again love affair. Simple and sweet, it borrows similar backing tracks from her previous "Why Doesn't Love Make Me Happy"—gently skittering percussions, soft strings, nervous, twittery guitars.

Crewe hoped the obvious similarity to the earlier Mary Hopkin hit would influence sales of "When Yesterday Was Tomorrow." The sheer audacity of the record itself—an evocative folk-style song on its top deck, a pretty, syrupy love ballad on its flip—should have been enough to get it recognized by disc jockeys and fans. But being quirky and trying to release a two-sided single that might appeal to two very different audiences seemed to shut itself out, and the record went nowhere.

The last shot at success didn't come for another four months. Lesley had to wait impatiently for Crewe to search for the hit that would rescue them both—one from radio poison, the other from bankruptcy. He unearthed what would become their final collaboration, an oddity of a single and probably the best of the Crewe recordings.

"Back Together" launched gospel music to hallucinatory heights. Backed by a howling church choir, a rousing revival-house stomp, hand-ripping claps, and a dash of country twang, Lesley praises the Lord for reuniting her with her past lost love, despite the skepticism of well-meaning but hurtful naysayers. Crewe recaptures the spunk and energy of "Sunshine, Lollipops, and Rainbows" while creating a neo-religious motif. Lesley's bright, ecstatic performance complemented the song's inherent, contagious enthusiasm, invoking an image of a sweltering, white-clapboard chapel in the humid, deep American south.

The flipside boasted a powerhouse ballad called "Quiet Love," about a warm and gentle man who asks for nothing, gives more than he takes, whose kindhearted presence is both minor and huge. "He's a little guy," Lesley sings, "a mountain high!" As an ironic turn on the title, Crewe's production is big, unreserved, and so dense in spots that instruments are impossible to tell apart. A ghostly sitar, soaring strings, empirical trumpets, an assembly of strumming guitars, and a resounding backing choir, all collide in a cascade of noise and echo that sounds like each component is competing for attention—an overall sound that rivals the very best of Phil Spector. The song fades away in a quiet, false ending, then returns, full blast, with the thundercloud roll of a timpani.

"Back Together" had been slated to appear on a soundtrack for the motion picture *Appleman*. But Crewe's run of bad luck would continue with the news that the film had been shelved, forcing him to release "Back Together" by itself in another vain attempt to see a financial return. Without the film as a context for the song, the unusual single simply baffled those who noticed it, then dropped from view.

The fate of Crewe's independent label was dismal. He couldn't sell his stars or his singles, regardless of the excellence of the tunes and the commitment of the artists. But no amount of perseverance could keep Crewe from filing for bankruptcy, and in only a year his outfit was shut down, taking with him the catalogue of existing recordings, as well as Lesley's lost Crewe recordings—a medley of "Hey Jude/Cry Me a River," "It Took a Long Time" (recorded in 1974 by LaBelle), and another "message" song, "Does Anybody Care About Tomorrow?" At the time of this writing, the Crewe recordings still have not seen a proper CD or digital release. Tracking down the original 45s may be difficult, but well worth the effort, as these seven rare tracks represent some of the very best of Gore's recorded material. The cuts run the full gamut of Crewe's genius, a showcase of his own eclectic and wide range of tastes, from elegance ("Why Doesn't Love Make Me Happy," "Why You, Why Me"), to social activism ("Tomorrow's Children"), to flamboyance ("Quiet Love," "Come Softly to Me") and even elements of camp ("Back Together").

In 1971, Lesley again was out of a contract, a label, or job propositions. New York didn't seem to offer anything anymore, except to stifle her attempts at further growth in her career. With the disintegration of Crewe records, Lesley decided there was nothing else binding her to the East Coast and moved back to sunny Southern California to reestablish herself. She was desperate to be taken seriously as a contemporary artist instead of what she was quickly becoming—Lesley Gore, has-been singer of malt shop memories.

# A BLANK PIECE OF PAPER AND A HOPE

It's almost incomprehensible to think that the girl who sold millions of records for Mercury, who was the youthful voice behind the classics "It's My Party," "Judy's Turn to Cry," "You Don't Own Me," "She's a Fool," and "California Nights," could be left with no money, no reserves. But that was the case in 1971—the teen superstar of the '60s had nothing left.

"I haven't really taken care of myself financially," Gore confessed in 2006, "and that's one of the things that I regret most. That's one of the things I am trying to deal with now." While her trusted father had managed her personal schedules, prescribed managers had handled the singer's monetary affairs. Her contract had entitled her to a 2 percent royalty that only grew in minuscule increments as she sold more records, but once Mercury deducted the cost of studio time, musicians, touring costs, payments to miscellaneous personnel, and what the label determined were "exorbitant fees" that the singer had incurred (if something was so much as Xeroxed, she was billed for it), there was simply no way Gore could have amassed the fortune one would have expected her vastly successful '60s career to have earned. "Anyone who thinks I could retire and buy a house in the South of France is badly mistaken," Lesley quipped to Alan Betrock. As a matter of fact, she had received one check in 1963 in the amount of $16,000—and that was it. But as a sixteen-year-old entering an environment she knew nothing about, she had no reason to suspect the worst of the people representing her. She wasn't even sure after it was recorded that "It's My Party" would see the light of day—Mercury president Irving Green had approached the young singer to soften the harsh possibility of an unissued single by saying, "Now, sweetheart, if this never gets released, I don't want you to be disappointed."

But Lesley was in good company; the same fiscal fate met other hit makers of the decade like Del Shannon ("Runaway") and Little Eva ("The Locomotion"), who received a lump sum once, then struggled for the duration of their careers. The Teen Queens, who hit big with "Eddie My Love," later plummeted into such despair that ten years after their massive record, both sisters would be dead of drugs and suicide. Imagine Madonna, Britney Spears, Taylor Swift, or Lady Gaga barely scraping by with their cavalcade of gigantic global hit songs, albums, and concerts.

But no one was directing the young artists back then, or offering sage advice, or guarding the best interests of the vulnerable female teen idols. In *Girl Groups*, author Alan Betrock shrewdly points out that the ruling powers behind the scenes would not have accrued their own fortunes or expanded their labels without the fresh, young talent they were exploiting—the happenstance "Iko Iko" wouldn't have seen vinyl if not for the Dixie Cups fooling around with some extra studio time; Phil Spector couldn't have built his empire without Ronnie Bennett; and Motown, or the Supremes for that matter, would not have registered with listeners as quickly or potently were it not for the Marvelettes and "Please Mr. Postman." In fact, artists wouldn't have been able to use their own famous names to tour if the Marvelettes and other artists of the Golden Era hadn't banded together in 1999 and convinced a court to rule in their favor to allow the original acts to continue using their groups' names to perform, and finally protect their shareholdings in the records that made a lot of other people a lot of money.

Several printed articles reveal Lesley's disdain for a record industry that she believed was a misogynistic atmosphere, a system that regularly kept women subjugated to lower rungs, both as artists and executives, which accounted for the ease with which it essentially robbed her of an income; in one hurtful irony, the songwriters of "You Don't Own Me" were awarded a souvenir gold record to hang on their walls, while the girl whose name became synonymous with the song received nothing.

The other artists on the label were predominately male, and it was clear, at least to Gore, that their only interest was in promoting and protecting their male stars. Music writer Richard Williams concurs, writing of the atmosphere of the early '60s, "Kids made the music, but they had no say-so in what happened to it after they had put their stuff on to the spool of magnetic tape [ . . . ] The kids made it and the kids bought it, but it was the cigar-chomping fatties who first took the cream, and then the milk, and finally threw the empty carton into the trash can."

Morris Diamond defends Mercury's management of Lesley, calling the notion of the label having taken advantage of her youth and inexperience "way off-base." "She got first-class treatment from all departments at Mercury," he told this author. "Lesley had nothing but the best in advisors, and her parents were very sharp and knowledgeable about the record business. I had the most respect for her as did Quincy and treated her accordingly. There were never any disputes about her earnings from the sales of 'It's My Party' that I'm aware of."

And as wonderful a friend as her producer had been to her, Lesley contended to Shauna Swartz, "Quincy Jones was a great mentor, but he was a man in a man's world." She vented her frustration not at the individuals who truly cared for her and navigated her career with genuine affection, but at the label as a corporate entity, an institution that sought to invest and protect its own interests. Surprisingly, it wasn't just the artists who felt suppressed by their labels, it was anyone considered a subordinate in the chain of command. Quincy Jones wrote in his autobiography, "The records sold millions, and I didn't get an extra dime. I'd signed a contract with Mercury that clearly stated that 'in *no* event'—and the word *no* was underlined—'will you make over $40,000 a year.' As VP, it had seemed okay to me at the time. Before then, I never knew what a producer was or did [ . . . ] I didn't know producers got percentages back then, but after Lesley's records sold millions, I learned quick."

Lesley had earned enough to cover her college education, for which she was certainly grateful. But there was little left beyond tuition on which to live, to sustain much of a comfortable life as an adult now aged out of the celebrity status she'd once known so well. Her move to the West Coast enabled her to enroll in songwriting courses with composer Dick Grove to fine-tune her craft, and to feel like she was still an artist. There were no club dates, no more stadiums of screaming fans, just oldies caravans making the rounds for audiences to come see how their favorite idols had aged and to hear the songs that had gotten them through the jungles and mine-fields of high school. "I had been to several record companies and was told that there was no room for new artists. They said their rosters were full," a dejected Gore told journalist Barbara Lewis in 1972 (Lewis, accidentally salting the open wound, misspelled the singer's name as "Leslie" throughout the entire article).

"I think I turned to [song]writing really just to wake up in the morning and be a musician and to have something to do, and feel like a musician everyday even if I wasn't working," Lesley told *AfterEllen* in 2005. "And that's what got me to the piano, that's what got me up in the morning—a blank piece of paper and a hope to have something by the end of the day."

The first songs she drafted on her own were awful. Lesley agreed in the same interview that this period was a struggle for her. "It always is, trying to self-motivate," she said. "I think it's the hardest thing a person can do."

And as dark as this time was, there were a couple glimmers of light during her nadir of despair. One was in the freedom to finally be herself. She reluctantly came out to her family and closest friends after a typewritten note was delivered to Gore's parents tattling that the singer had been spotted going into a gay nightspot, and to her relief, she remained close to all of them, particularly to brother Michael. They spoke constantly and continued to write songs together. He helped alleviate her fears of being totally alone, and silenced the terror of coming out and coming to terms with her sexuality, a process Gore told the *Lesbian News* was "a very long, a very tedious, and a very soul-searching experience."

In 1969, having returned from a tour in Australia, Lesley met jewelry designer Lois Sasson through a mutual friend. The singer had brought back an opal from the land down under that she wanted made into a ring, and Lesley—a jewel herself in search of the perfect setting—struck up a friendship with Lois that quickly became something much more personal and intimate. Theirs was a brief but spectacular affair, which had tapered to an end by the time Lesley had fled New York for California in what became a quest to find herself and restore the music. But the relationship with Lois, fleeting though passionate, helped Lesley to discover her center, finally bringing the complete human being out of the recesses of the closet and into the golden sunlight of self-acceptance and security. Though Ronny struggled with revelation and said so—she had different expectations and envisioned an entirely different kind of life for her daughter—Lois told *Closer Weekly* that Lesley "was totally comfortable in her sexual shoes."

The second ray of hope in the early '70s came in the form of actress Ellen Weston, who immediately befriended the castaway Gore. Born in April 1939, Weston grew up in New York and moved westward to pursue a career in acting. The spritely, doe-eyed actress (who bore a slight resemblance to Gore) had a recurring role as Dr. Steele on TV's *Get Smart*, and made notable appearances in many of the most popular programs of the '70s like *SWAT* and *Rod Serling's Night Gallery*. Eventually she would use her multiple skills as a force behind the scenes, writing and producing for telefilms and TV series for decades.

Ellen had met Lesley briefly in the early '60s; Weston had just finished an evening performance on Broadway in the play, *Mary, Mary*, when her husband bailed on their planned dinner because he had some work to do with music producer Quincy Jones. He invited her to come along, and that's when Ellen first saw "the kid" who was responsible for the hit records everyone was talking about (though Weston would confess that, as a classically trained musician, she was one of the few around a radio at the time who had never heard of Johnny or Judy).

When the two ladies met again some ten years later, they combined into a dynamic songwriting duo. Weston had asked Gore to perform the lead in a promotional demonstration of a musical she'd written, and Gore, charmed by the lyrics, asked if Weston would be interested in pooling their talents. Together they would create a stellar sixty original songs. The meshing of Lesley's musical know-how with Ellen's genius as a wordsmith was seamless. They peddled some of their material to producer Joe Porter at Motown's Los Angeles arm, Mowest. He liked what he heard—clever, sometimes downright moving songs, interpreted with sincerity and maturity by a grown-up pop idol. Wanting to extend the new label to white artists and reach a broader audience, Porter invited Lesley back into the recording studio and polished up a dozen tracks to release her first complete album in nearly five years.

The finished LP, *Someplace Else Now*, begins with the introductory "For Me" and ends in the epilogue "For You." The ten songs in between tell a tightly woven story that, listened to in order, reveal a woman's journey from loneliness, to love, to loss, to acceptance, and finally to independence and personal reconciliation. The narrative drive lithely and deftly springs between anticipation, joy, crippling pain and disappointment, and ultimately wends into peace. The record was as far away from Lesley's girl-group days as the Doors were from Shelley Fabares.

*Someplace Else Now* is stripped of the noise and clatter of traditional pop music, and is instead infused with a simple folk and country ambiance. The crisp, bare style intensifies the strength and integrity of the songs themselves, and the overall tone of the album is distinctly feminine and raw with controlled emotion, running completely against the grain of her previous Mercury-polished gems.

The opening remarks of "For Me" welcome back fans, promising something new and bold. "Know me," she sings in a whisper, "I've always been there / I'll take you places you've never been." The album transitions smoothly into "The Road I Walk," a gospel-flavored track whose melody and piano backing are reminiscent of "Amazing Grace," before building into a horn and tambourine chorus backed by a female choir that echoes Gore's lyric, similar to the call-and-response style of the church. The road she walks in the title is a quest for knowledge, for understanding the meaning of a journey rife with sadness and riddled with tribulations.

"The Road I Walk" is followed by the bitter and scathing "Out of Love," where tenuous emotional bonds stretch and snap in examples of love gone wrong—between a miserable father and mother, between embattled siblings, and between lovers whose earlier passions have been dulled by monotony and lies. A snarling Gore sets a malevolent tone in the song's early measures, and the cynical lyrics seem to dare listeners that if this is what love is all about, who the hell needs it?

Perhaps the album's finest track is the countrypolitan "She Said That," which tells the story of a luckless woman who "chose the wrong apartment" and watches her life slip by in inches, a lonely character who fixes up her face and waits for no one to show up. She had decided to save her love for one person, but discovers, much too late, that she wasted her life on a daydream. The song is all the more powerful by Lesley's repeated insistence that "that was she, not me," as if desperately trying to convince herself—as well as we voyeuristic listeners—that she is nothing like the woman in the story. At the end of the track, the nameless woman has ended her life and earns validation at last as clucking neighbors suggest it was probably for the best that she died. Lesley internalizes the plight of the tragic figure and both laments, and separates herself from, the woman's death in the song's closing lines. The emotional pull of the track is brought closer to listeners in its intimate arrangement—the deftly blended acoustic guitars, gently bleating trumpets, and pensive violins.

The upbeat "Don't Wanna Be One" is a neat little pure pop song that captures the bounce and frivolity of her earlier hits with a mellower backbeat. But finding true love and keeping it is never stronger than it is in "Be My Life." Slow and deep, the singer pleads with her lover to be anything and everything, but most importantly, to share her life with her. The beautiful lyrics fill the big sound of the track—a church organ, a full background choir that provides a skyline to Lesley's lead vocals, and a certain sense of majesty makes "Be My Life" sound as if it had been recorded in an echoing, big city cathedral.

The next track, written with Michael Gore, domesticates the newfound love in "Where Do You Go (When You Get Home)," where life falls into a steady and cozy routine, and "home is the journey that lies ahead." The performance and lyrics are both shy, as two lives intertwine and each finds a rhythm in a delicate dance of togetherness.

The mood of the album suddenly turns blue with "What Did I Do Wrong," sort of the "first quarrel" in the narrative of the album, where a betrayed Lesley demands an explanation for the painful rejection from her "wild and careless" lover. She nearly sobs at her lover's firm decision to choose the freedom of being single over the commitment of being with, and loving, Lesley.

Moving beyond soiled past loves, the album's title track places the singer in a place of both understanding and uncertainty, of resolve and tentativeness. Gore sings wistfully, "Time and living showed me how" to ease softly into the present, "and took me someplace else now." Gore continues the theme of coming to terms with the here and now, with "tomorrow's todays," in the next track, "Mine," which contends that nothing is more fearful than realizing a momentous epiphany, "The truth that only two can know as one and I know more each day / Love's the hardest game to play."

The last complete song on the album is "No Sad Songs," where fear and doubt are finally banished for a much-deserved happy ending, that pain leads to experience, and experience results in wisdom. She knows this way, she sings with confidence, "And now we're moving on."

Like "For Me" at the start of the record, "For You" provides the opposite bookend, almost like offering sage advice to a parting fellow journeyman, an epitaph to listeners: "For today you've been with me / dreaming my way," and Gore wishes her listeners a kindred spirit with whom to continue the adventure.

From its graceful opening, through the chasms of emotional experiences explored, to its quiet, introspective conclusion, *Someplace Else Now* is Lesley Gore's unequivocal masterpiece—the finest, most assured and perfect album of her career. And, by keeping the object of her desires in the songs gender-neutral—replacing the ubiquitous "he" and "him" with the use of the objective, omnipresent "you"—this record was her most honest endeavor and could resonate with any listener in any type of relationship. Nestled somewhere in between Carole King's earth mother persona, the gritty, hard edges of Carly Simon, and the mellow adult-contemporary crooning of Karen Carpenter, the album would induct Gore into the pantheon of remarkable female singer-songwriters.

Joe Porter fixed what previous producers had gotten wrong. The days of releasing 45s, then slapping together LPs full of filler to capitalize on the hit singles, were over. The Beatles had taught American acts that the fullest expression of art is in the totality of the album, with singles released later to uphold the integrity of the complete body of work. And now, with the disintegration of the Beatles, an epoch had ended; the Top 40's love affair with all things British had finally run its course like the girl-group era that came before it, prompting American singers to stampede back onto the charts.

*Someplace Else Now* was released in July 1972, and sales were almost instantly stagnant. Mowest, busy with multiple projects and faltering out on the West Coast, far away—perhaps too far—from its Detroit life source, did little to market the album beyond releasing its only single, "She Said That," in late October. Longtime fans relished the fresh comeback, and most reviews of the album were respectful. *Billboard* commented, "The hitmaker of the '60s debuts on Mowest with a totally fresh, unique, meaningful approach as a composer-performer, and she's right up to date. This should prove a new career and following for her." But not all commentaries were friendly, such as Shannon Jewell's slightly testy review of one of Gore's live

**TOP 10 SINGLES
JULY 1972***

#1  Lean On Me
Bill Withers

#2  Too Late to Turn Back Now
Cornelius Bros.
& Sister Rose

#3  Daddy Don't You Walk So
Fast
Wayne Newton

#4  (If Loving You Is Wrong)
I Don't Wanna Be Right
Luther Ingram

#5  Outa-Space
Billy Preston

#6  Song Sung Blue
Neil Diamond

#7  Brandy (You're a Fine Girl)
Looking Glass

#8  Rocket Man
Elton John

#9  Alone Again (Naturally)
Gilbert O'Sullivan

#10  How Do You Do?
Mouth & McNeal

*From Dave McAleer's *Book of Hit Singles*

performances while promoting the album: "She's very, very tiny for such a powerful voice, although the raspiness borders on irritating when she reaches for the upper registers [ . . . ] Her stage personality is not the warmest. There is very little chatter between numbers, but she's still very good from the nostalgia standpoint at least."

And then, suddenly, far too quickly, *Someplace Else Now* was gone, and the commercial flop did nothing to win Lesley the respect and identity she craved as a successful songwriter. She was crushed by its failure, and her peers tried their best to defend it. Her manager, Dick Fox, loved the album but was irritated that the industry was quick to dismiss Gore's talents simply because of her status of a kitschy '60s throwback. Composer Marvin Hamlisch, who adored the new album, agreed with Fox's assessment, claiming that his friend Lesley was capable of so much more than her teenybopper caricature would allow. Phil Ramone also concurred and told this author, "They didn't want who Lesley Gore had become, they wanted the one who used to be." Ronnie Spector posted online that Gore "had a certain sound. But you want to be able to do new things too, and it can be hard on an artist that is so identified with a certain sound." Legendary Paul Anka, who managed to find steady footing in the '70s, still told another writer, "Unfortunately, the infrastructure of our business is such that people don't allow you to make that radical a change."

In a crisis of confidence, and with bills to pay, Lesley Gore had no other choice but to step back in time, dust off the teen music that made her famous, and hitch a ride on the nostalgia bandwagon.

# THAT OLD TIME ROCK AND ROLL

By the mid-'70s, America was in the midst of another musical shift. Having outgrown their infatuation with mop-topped British acts and not on the fringe enough to absorb and enjoy the psychedelic groups, many mainstream listeners decided to check in with their former favorite singers and revisit the hits that reminded them of cruising down Main Street and dancing at the candy stores. Fans rode a wave of nostalgia made suddenly popular by the colossal TV hits *Happy Days* and its offshoot *Laverne and Shirley*, as well as *Sha Na Na*, the cheesy variety show that invited Golden Age idols to make appearances in the spotlight again, singing the songs that had once made them famous (Gore, sporting a tight Shari Lewis perm, would appear on the show to sing "You Don't Own Me").

Former disc jockey Richard Nader was one of those dissatisfied by the AM radio trends that were alienating young adult listeners and their displaced heroes now aging into their thirties. He sought to bring back the rock music and idols he missed by grouping the artists into touring packages. Nader couldn't sell his idea to promoters, who considered his heroes washed-up. He even tried cajoling Dick Clark, who, shockingly, didn't see the value in drudging up the dusty jukebox acts that had made his *American Bandstand* a cultural institution. In 1969, Nader finally scraped up $35,000 of his own to rent the Felt Forum at Madison Square Garden, then went about the daunting task of recruiting solo artists and reuniting splintered groups who had moved on with their lives—some worse than others.

"Bo Diddley was working in a restaurant attached to a garage because his car had broken down, and he couldn't afford to get it repaired," Nader's wife, Deborah, told the *New York Times*. Nader even paid out of pocket to dress his reassembled bands in matching suits. The bargain paid off, as the shows at the Garden were sold-out sensations, and the performances had to be transplanted from the Forum to the Garden's main arena to accommodate the explosion in attendance. The concerts resuscitated such varied performers as Chuck Berry, Kathy Young and Jimmy Clanton; girl groups like the Shirelles and the Crystals; doo-wop heartthrobs like the Five Satins and the Coasters; and early pioneers Bill Hailey and His Comets, and the Platters.

Nader told a newspaper in 1973 that audiences, totaling half a million fans within the first few years of the rock revival, had returned in droves for "their own memories and associations [ ... ] They were getting back into the irresponsibility, the carefreeness, the fun they had before they got married." Retro was cool, and vintage sounded fresh and incomparable.

Buoyed by the success of Nader's shows and his obvious admiration of, and respect for, the singers of the '50s and '60s, Lesley, who had resisted the memoryfests, signed on to join the nostalgia tours. Her first performance in the spring of 1975 was such a tremendous success, she signed on for another show at the Garden—where, for the second time, her name helped pack in a second sell-out performance for 19,000 fans.

Running on the momentum of her renewed popularity, Lesley made the bold choice to appear alone as a solo act at nightclubs and smaller arenas. To her shock and delight, she drew such crowds that one venue in Atlanta, Georgia, all but forced her to hold over the performances for a lengthier stay. These independent tours also allowed her to audition new material to an audience; the old hits brought in the fans who were held captive while she mixed fresh songs into the fold. The balance was a delicate one, and she understood the tradeoff. "There is no point in me getting up on a stage and not doing 'It's My Party,'" she acknowledged to Shauna Swartz. "There's every reason to do it. Where do you want to be: your career before or your career now? Well, they're the same thing. It's my career, it's my life, it's my work in progress." To "broaden her foundation," the singer consented, "I do all the songs people expect me to do, and then hopefully I give them a little something extra."

And as long as the new, original songs came buttressed with "It's My Party" and "She's a Fool," fans were receptive to the music they never would have expected. One reviewer commented that the best songs she heard Gore perform one evening at a show in Cleveland were not the usual "oldies," but three dramatic songs composed by the singer: "Golden Couple," about the unraveling of a seemingly perfect relationship; "Other Lady," concerning a wife suspecting her husband's infidelity; and "Child," which celebrates the bond between parents and their kids. The recognition must have been thrilling for Lesley, who commented in the same interview, "You've got to realize your task at hand. There's no point in alienating your fan base. What I think you want to do is bring them along and then pick up a few more people along the way. So, can you be bitter and make that choice? Sure you can, but it's not the one that I feel comfortable with."

In the mid-'70s, she appeared at the Reno Sweeney, one of New York's hippest cabaret clubs. Fans in the East were delighted to invite the thirty-year-old back home, where a more sophisticated, reinvented Lesley introduced a decidedly more adult act that consisted of "reimagined" versions of her classics, woven together with songs penned by Gore and Weston. Her two-week engagement at the cabaret was sold out, prompting the Reno Sweeney to invite her back the following year, where she repeated the success of the first engagement. Weston recalled to Edward Eckstine that during one of these appearances, "Something very strange used to happen when [Lesley] was performing [ ... ] It was as if the audience was watching [her] reach into [herself] and pull out one wonderful thing after another."

The singer who had been forgotten about and rejected just a couple of years before was now filling clubs to their capacities and stepping offstage to rousing standing ovations. The rehabilitated interest in Lesley Gore and her music did not go ignored by the recording industry, which kept track of the packed crowds and glowing reviews that the singer garnered in her trek across the United States. From New York to Los Angeles with several major cities in between, the praise for her live performances was unanimous: "Her infections and timbre are under perfect musical control," wrote one trade columnist, while another, hyperbolic commentator offered, "She has more voice, more meaning, more magnetism in one number than Helen Reddy has ever achieved."

To capitalize on her resurrected fame, A&M Records signed Gore for a one-year contract. Founded in 1962 by musician Herb Alpert and promoter Jerry Moss (who helped propel the Crests' "Sixteen Candles" into rock history), the independent label set up shop at the Charlie Chaplin Studios at 1416 North LeBrea Avenue in Hollywood. They started strong by producing records by Alpert and his instrumental band, the Tijuana Brass, then firmly planted the label onto the pop charts by guiding such acts as Joe Cocker, Cat Stevens, and the Carpenters. By the 1970s, A&M often dominated the Top 20 lists thanks to performers like Billy Preston ("Nothing From Nothing"), Bazuka ("Dynomite"), Nazareth ("Love Hurts"), and most regularly, Captain & Tennille ("Love Will Keep Us Together"). It's also interesting to note that by this time, with only a few exceptions, the Mercury label was making fewer appearances near the top of the charts.

As well received as her live performances had been, Lesley was still nervous about attempting such a lofty venture; the failure and sadness over *Someplace Else Now* were never far from her mind, her unexorcized demons. Some consolation came in the fact that a few of her contemporaries had bounced back big once the British invasion had dissipated. Paul Anka hit #1 in 1974 with "You're Having My Baby," and Neil Sedaka scored the top spot twice in 1975 with "Laughter In The Rain" and "Bad Blood." The biggest difference, though, was that Anka and Sedaka were men, both powerful figures in popular music, and Gore had no illusions that the male-heavy record industry would be any kinder or any more supportive to her as a woman with fewer recording options to her name. Men could age and dignify; women were not allowed to.

And making Lesley's partnership with A&M even sweeter was being reunited with her old friend and former producer, Quincy Jones. He recalled a day when the ladies brought him some of their demos on tape that "blew me out the door, and Lesley sat down at the piano and played me some more that put the icing on the cake. That's when we decided to do it again," he told Edward Eckstine in the mid-'70s. The press-ballyhooed pairing generated excitement for their project, and a year later, Lesley's ninth studio album—*Love Me By Name*—was released in high hopes of becoming a sizable hit, and hoisting the singer back into wider national attention.

# DISCO

*Love Me By Name* definitely had Quincy Jones's signature all over the finished project: the rich, layered orchestrations, the experimentation with synthesized effects then in vogue, and a fresh American sound that merged pop, funk, and disco. The nine tracks, all composed by Lesley and Ellen (but credited playfully to "Lil' Bits & The Witch" in the album's liner notes), are lively, radio-friendly, and, with a contemporary sound engineered by Jones, commercial. While the artistic *Someplace Else Now* defied tidy categories, *Love Me By Name* would be glossy, sparkly pure pop.

First, Jones assembled a crack team of musicians to give the album its flare. He recruited his own find, the Brothers Johnson (George and Louis, who would score their own funk hits "I'll Be Good To You" and "Stomp"), to helm the lead guitars and basses. Herbie Hancock, Dave Grusin, and Quincy Jones were among the eight that banged out the keyboard riffs and synthesizers. Toots Thielemans made his heavy presence known with his masterful harmonica solos. And "handclaps" were credited to Lesley, Ellen, Quincy, and engineer Larry Quinn.

Similar to Jones's earlier contributions to Gore's recordings, the music is tight, focused, and polished. Tapping into the success of George McCrae ("Rock Your Baby"), Barry White ("Can't Get Enough of Your Love, Babe"), Carol Douglas ("Doctor's Orders"), and KC and the Sunshine Band ("That's the Way I Like It"), the album's first track is the supremely disco "Sometimes." It's a powerful introduction to the rest of the record—danceable, with Gore's voice reaching sultry lows and soaring highs against a beat that is throbbing and breathless, "Sometimes" could compete with any Gloria Gaynor or Donna Summer single.

A homicidal butcher, a coworker turned assassin, and police officers on the prowl in the middle of the night comprise the creepy cast of characters in "Paranoia," a great rocker in the vein of Creedence Clearwater Revival's "Bad Moon Rising," replete with growling lyrics and guitars that screech and whine like back-alley cats. Another high-octane song on the album is "Immortality," which pokes fun at Lesley's past and honors the notch made in pop music by her old records. "Carve my name, 'I Love You, Johnny' / on the summer house stair," she sings, evoking the foggy memory of Johnny and Judy with tongue-in-cheek jab. In an ode to her current career standing (and a prophetic nod to the end of her life), she punches a line toward the end of the track about leaving her coffin lid slightly ajar and hanging a sign on her tombstone that says she'll "be back in a minute." The album's upbeat cuts draw in the casual listener, then caresses them with songs more sensual, more riveting.

Gore and Company slow the pace with a few mellow pieces. Another paean to the past is the lovely "Can't Seem to Live Our Good Times Down," where a melancholy Gore clings to the trinkets and souvenirs of a long lost love—a cache of photographs depicting the smiling, mugging couple; revisiting their favorite places along the boulevard; and even the rough times that the singer admits she can't recall as well through her rose-tinted memories.

"Along the Way" boasts some of Gore's and Weston's most poignant, poetic word wizardry. The introspective track muses on the lives that enter and exit along the way, those interpersonal exchanges, both brief and prolonged, that shape and contribute to a human life. Among its final verses, telling of a journey of experience nearing its end, "I turned just once to see / what all the fuss had been about," and discovered who she was, as well as who she could never become. Though both singer and songwriter were only in their early thirties, the lyrics suggest a wisdom, a philosophical outlook on life and death and what it might all be about, well beyond the young women's years.

"Don't Stop Me"—a more lighthearted, teasing version of "You Don't Own Me"—reveals a singer simply shrugging off the complaints, criticism, and conventions of well-meaning but clueless people around her. "I'll put aside my funny ways and hide my lunacy," Gore sings, but adds the provisional, "If you can tell me what's so great about reality." In another possible nod to her own sexuality, and to fans with ears tuned to pick up the cues between beats and measures, the singer jokes about having to suppress a secret smile when her lover turns off the light, deciding that she can search for love in other corners.

During her cross-country touring in the mid-'70s, one of the songs Gore had introduced to audiences was "Other Lady," which survived to make the cut on the album. Far from Johnny's teenaged scheming and cheating at the birthday party, a sadness resonates from within "Other Lady," as the story of infidelity between adults takes on a pain and depression that deepens with age, as the relationships become harder to maintain and harder to lose. The song captures the betrayal, the bitterness, the fear of that awkward moment when the two women must eventually pass one another in the streets of their hometown, and finally, the ultimate acceptance that both women will be destroyed by the man who has dragged them all into a devastating situation; the defeated singer decides the two ladies can only call a truce, as the philandering man needs one of them for pleasure, the other for sustenance—and the vicious circle feeds them all.

The tender "Give It to Me, Sweet Thing," is a gospel-hued love song backed by a gently pleading electronic piano, a weeping saxophone, a lush, romantic sweep of strings, and a soulful church choir.

Completing the collection is the title track, "Love Me By Name," which appears twice as a full-length song and as a reprise to conclude the album (at every opportunity, Quincy Jones enthusiastically told interviewers and writers that "Love Me By Name" was one of his favorite songs). It sounds like nothing else on the album, an eerie ballad set against wobbly chimes, space-aged sounding whistles sliding up and down digital scales, sounding both ahead of its time and '70s time-stamped. Lesley sings of rolling out of someone else's bed and into the harsh white glare of daylight, feeling guilty about the tryst, knowing this wasn't what she wanted for herself, to flee—used and spent—from a lover who didn't bother to learn her name the night before. When she finally meets a person who has taken "the sweet time to ask about me," the singer's response is an almost orgasmic, pleading, jubilant demand to love her by name, and not discard her into anonymity—a plea that could have been made of her fans.

*Love Me By Name* was released in May 1976 with Lesley's dedication scribed in the liner notes: "This album is dedicated with love to my friends Dick Fox, The King, and Ellen Weston, The Nibbler." The critical accolades were immediate and satisfying; another major comeback for Lesley Gore, Disco Diva, seemed well on its way. *Billboard* was the first to succinctly sing the album's praises: "Excellent LP, keyed by more versatility than the artist showed in all her days of big Top 40 hits [ . . . ] Strong singing [ . . . ] Fine production from Quincy Jones, but the real star is Lesley, who developed into a real stylist, writes well [ . . . ] and could easily move back to the pop forefront." Not to be beaten, *Variety* piggybacked a week later, "Lesley Gore returns, writing the music, too [ . . . ] There's a lot of production, much of it by Quincy Jones, in what is often an excellent album."

Writing for *Crawdaddy*, reviewer Toby Goldstein added in August 1976, "To the relief of nostalgia freaks, Lesley Gore is still singing about love, and with perfect tear-jerking flair. She has learned the value of controlling her runaway fury, not exploding too often but saving her excitement for points of emphasis [ . . . ] *Love Me By Name* displays Lesley's new Cabaret Style guided once again by Quincy Jones's horns, handclaps, and strings. She may never speak so directly to the hordes of agonizing adolescents as in 1963, but the 1976 Lesley Gore is a favorite voice returned, polished, and, these days, comfortably listenable."

Perhaps the best (and wittiest) analysis came from *Boston*'s Don Shewey: "Yes, it's Judy's turn to cry, because Lesley Gore has grown up from her bitchy teenager days to become an elegant singer/songwriter of star quality [ ... ] Lesley's collaborations with lyricist Ellen Weston are considerably more substantial than the plastic pop of the '60s. What comes as a shock is the range and sophistication of Lesley's gorgeous voice, which rivals Terry Garthwaite's for color and flexibility. At least half the credit for the high quality of *Love Me By Name*, however, must go to producer Quincy Jones, whose lavish and lively arrangements envelop the tunes like a mink coat on Liz Taylor [ ... ] The result is a classy album of topnotch music from start to finish."

The mirror-ball-and-confetti welcome by critics of Gore's new sound wasn't right away matched by fans. The album's first single, "Immortality" (backed with "Give It to Me Sweet Thing"), had been released in June 1975 to deaf ears. The single had seen some action across the Atlantic in England, so Quincy was sure the project had some fight in it.

To promote the completed album in the summer of 1976, Jones released "Sometimes" as a single to cash in on its modern disco style. Gore also made the rounds trying to sell the new record, and took a gamey approach on her tours, making teasing jokes about her sexuality to accepting crowds in San Francisco theaters. A writer from the *Advocate* recalled Gore opening one of her acts by punning Elton John's hit song, telling the audience, "Don't let your

---

**TOP 10 SINGLES
MAY 1976***

#1  Welcome Back
    John Sebastian

#2  Fooled Around and Fell
    in Love
    Elvin Bishop

#3  Silly Love Songs
    Wings

#4  Boogie Fever
    The Sylvers

#5  Love Hangover
    Diana Ross

#6  Get Up and Boogie
    Silver Convention

#7  Right Back Where We
    Started From
    Maxine Nightingale

#8  Shannon
    Henry Gross

#9  Show Me the Way
    Peter Frampton

#10 Tryin' to Get the
    Feeling Again
    Barry Manilow

*From Dave McAleer's *Book of
Hit Singles*

son go down on me." Gay fans, historically more open to new, avant-garde acts as well as hoisting autumnal legends like Eartha Kitt and Peggy Lee up onto pedestals (and keeping them performing), embraced their old pal Lesley Gore—whose repertoire of unreachable, cruel boys made her every gay boy's "fag hag" of the '60s, long before the term was coined—and helped to propel "Sometimes" to #8 on the Disco Chart, which had been created in response to the quickly and enormously popular musical trend that welcomed both black and female singers into the mainstream pop chart. *Creem*, delighted by Gore's return and open persona, contributed a perky and equally teasing commentary in 1977: "Beaming through the backbeat ether, her hair casting aside the world in butch-wax weariness, Lesley Gore still sings out of the side of her mouth—one of her well kept secrets of rock ascension. Just watch Brian Wilson any time he walks, talks, burps, it's all from the corner of the orifice. Lesley asks us to call her by name, and why not? She's still the heavy-metal chanteuse so many have tried and failed to become. This is a good record [and] it equates to a shutout in hockey."

But the glowing reviews and the showy performances couldn't save the drowning sales of *Love Me By Name*. Several key factors led to its brisk, but undeserving, demise. First was the overcommitment of producer Quincy Jones. By the mid-'70s, Jones's career was lava hot and spreading the man in various creative directions. His own album, *Mellow Madness*, was released in 1975 and streaked all the way up to #16 on the album charts. He also had the heavy task of writing the score for the television event film, *Roots*, which was only a year away from airing. At home, Jones and his second wife, Peggy Lipton, had just brought home their second daughter together, Rashida (who would go on to create two memorable TV characters for the NBC shows *The Office* and *Parks and Recreation*). Lesley's album was simply not priority, causing the record to take a year to complete. To make matters worse, Lesley's contract came up for renewal before the record was finished, and since executives at A&M had heard nothing of Gore's progress during the lapsed timeline, they decided prematurely to release the singer from the label.

Even if Jones hadn't been so distracted during the *Love Me By Name* project, the record suffered from a sense of the grandiose, as Gore's vocals are sometimes buried beneath the dense instrumentals and backing choirs. The personal, introspective, emotional conversation between the singer and listeners of *Someplace Else Now* is lost to Jones's panache for indulgent orchestrations on *Love Me by Name*, a criticism also hurled by *Variety*: "At times the production is a bit overwhelming and listeners could do with more Gore and less background music."

And there is always the second-guessing that comes from wondering what would have happened if four songs left off the album had been included—would that have made the difference between a flop and a phenomenon? Recorded but unreleased were "The Golden Couple" and "Child," which both received praise from audiences and reviewers when Gore performed them at clubs across the nation. Also missing were "I'd Like to Be" and a harder, juiced-up version of the breezy "Along the Way." Could any of these have met the middle-of-the-road listeners in their comfort zones better than "Sometimes" or "Immortality"?

It wouldn't be fair to rest all of the blame for the album's failure on the solid shoulders of Quincy Jones. Fans, simply, were a fickle kind of animal. They packed venues to see Gore perform the old hits, while open to hearing some new material thrown into the mix of oldies but goodies. But this same positive, symbiotic relationship did not attract audiences when the formula was reversed; Gore couldn't draw them in on the strength of her new music alone. They loved her best when she sang about adolescent angst, not when the singer was waxing poetic about the hazards of adult relationships and the complexities of life, not when the sometimes painful themes hit too close to home for the now thirty-somethings struggling with careers and marriages and mortgages, not when Lesley's new material came wrapped in the clutter of disco trappings—a fad itself that was only a year away from being demolished in a public, brutal backlash.

The final insulting turn of the screw came several years later when the cover sleeve of *Love Me by Name*—Gore is reaching forward holding a glowing orb of light, while her nude, airbrushed torso morphs into silver armor from the chest down, which must have seemed like a terribly modern design for its time—was included among one music website's embarrassing list of the "Fifty Worst Album Covers."

In 1978, further away from her old hits and still sore from the let-down of another major studio album, Gore recorded the unreleased track, "If Our Songs Still Make It (Why Can't We)," a love-gone-wrong song with a bitter delivery barely hidden beneath its upbeat, near-disco spunk. The clever, metaphorical lyrics describe a relationship, like a certain former hit record, that's "gone out of style," a passion hoping that it might "hit the charts once more." In the chorus, when Lesley yearns to "go back to sixty-three," the tune's commentary seems to be just as easily, if unintentionally, directed at Gore's failure to return to mainstream musical success as it is at the symbolic failed couple in the lyric's narrative. "Things can be as great as they were then," she ends longingly, and for the artist who spent years trying to expunge her gooey bubblegum image, 1963 suddenly seemed like a blissful but lost, irrevocable candyland.

Though far from reaching the art and craft that was *Someplace Else Now*, *Love Me by Name*, as commercially viable as it could have been, was still a remarkable collection of interesting pop music that showcased Gore's modern sensibilities, her chameleon ability to adopt and comfortably own current trends in music to stay alive. And survival now, as it was just a couple of years before, was key again. With a spectacularly failed major comeback, no hit records, and no contract in the foreseeable future, Lesley Gore was right back where she had started.

Track Thirteen

# THAT'S ENTERTAINMENT

The lost Crewe singles, *Someplace Else Now*, *Love Me by Name*, and any further prospects on the West Coast were dead and buried along with the '70s. Lesley's family and closest friends were in New Jersey and New York. And jewelry designer Lois Sasson, with whom the singer had entered into a whirlwind affair, was in the Big Apple. While it seemed like an easy choice to return back East, the impetus to move didn't happen until Michael Gore called up his sister in 1979 and enticed her back to New York with a great idea.

Michael had developed his own illustrious career in music, behind the scenes, scoring songs for motion pictures. Film director Alan Parker had approached Michael about the soundtrack for his new project, *Hot Lunch*, a coming-of-age story that follows a group of teenagers led by Bruno Martelli (portrayed by Lee Curreri) and Coco Hernandez (Irene Cara) and their interwoven stories while attending the New York High School of Performing Arts. Though not originally intended as a musical, especially since the heyday of Hollywood musical films had died out in the late '60s in favor of grittier, grimier filmmaking in the '70s, Michael had come up with some original material that he thought might be ideal for the characters in Parker's movie. The director was pleased and, inspired by the phenomenal success of the 1978 screen adaptation of the musical *Grease*, agreed with Michael that *Hot Lunch* had the potential to forge ahead as a realistic drama with a backbeat.

The soundtrack boasts several exceptional tracks: "Red Light," the sweet "Is It Okay If I Call You Mine," "Never Alone," and the commanding "I Sing the Body Electric." Ultimately, Michael's standout song would be "Fame," which later became the title of the film after Alan Parker, while strolling down 42nd Street in New York one afternoon, passed an adult movie theater that was showing a porno-graphic flick by the name of *Hot Lunch*.

Missing his sister, and having always respected her prowess for songwriting, Michael convinced Lesley to come back East to help him flesh out the film's score. She contributed the rousing, frantic "Hot Lunch Jam," and the dizzying "Out Here On My Own," which would become Coco's emotional torch song.

And she seemed to find a kindred spirit in the fictional Coco and her experiences. Lesley had certainly channeled much of herself—her isolation, failures, and uncertainties—into what is perhaps the film's most personal, moving lyric that conveys a sense of loneliness, a struggle to stay afloat in the maelstrom of a life upside down, and a longing to find one's place and connect to another human being. Irene Cara's performance in the film is riveting and flawless, both painful and hopeful.

*Fame* was released in May 1980, and everyone involved was re-warded with a smash movie, a formidable list of accolades and honors, and the pride of having participated in a watershed moment in film history—*Fame* ushered in a new era of big-screen musicals, including *Best Little Whorehouse in Texas*, *Little Shop of Horrors*, and *A Chorus Line*. *Fame* would also transition to the small screen in the form of a long-running TV series that premiered in 1982 and lasted six seasons. It spawned a 1997 television spin-off (*Fame L.A.*, which barely survived one season); it loaned its title to a 2003 television talent competition in the vein of *American Idol*; and it was resur-rected for the big screen in a critically panned 2009 remake. Of all the incarnations of *Fame*, its best and most fitting was the stage adaptation that was performed around the world to great acclaim.

In 1980, Irene Cara's cover of the titular song rocketed to #4, and earned the singer two Grammy nominations (for Best New Female Vocalist and Best New Pop Vocalist) and a Golden Globe nomination for Best Actress in a Musical; and the movie's other single, "Out Here on My Own," became a substantial hit at #19.

*Fame* proved to be one of the darlings of that season's Academy Award celebration, where it enjoyed multiple nominations for Best

Original Screenplay, Best Sound, and Best Editing. Lesley's "Out Here on My Own" was nominated for Best Song, but that trophy would go to her brother for "Fame," along with a second statuette for his Best Original Music Score, giving baby brother bragging rights over his older sister. The stature of the wins would send more work Michael's way; he would go on to score some of the decade's best loved films like *Terms of Endearment* (for which the Academy would honor Michael with another nomination for Best Score) and *Pretty in Pink*.

But not bringing home the award in that category was far from disappointing for Lesley. Her name was again at the forefront of the public's mind, and she shined as she proved to both television viewers and industry heavyweights how much she'd matured and developed professionally since her love triangle with Johnny and Judy—consummation at last for the undervalued songwriter.

When two Tauruses combine, the mix can be volatile. A stubborn and defiant sign, a Taurus will stand by their opinion with tiger tenacity, and pitting one against the other is a spectacle worthy of selling tickets to watch. At the same time, because a Taurus values commitment and solidarity, the joining of the two brings each contentment and emotional security. Returning to New York brought Lesley and Lois Sasson—another obstinate Bull—back together. They renewed their relationship, setting up house soon after reconnecting, and found the relationship was as sensual and exhilarating as when they first met.

"Because I sometimes live in a dream world, one of the things that Lois has made me do is actually face the problems," Gore told Denise Penn in 2006. "That's half the battle right there; if you face a problem, or acknowledge it, then you must do something about it. So she is a little bit more pragmatic than I am." She was grateful for Lois's return not only because of the fulfilling friendship and companionship Lois brought into her life, but for the sense of balance and organization that artists—an admittedly flighty, unfocused kind of animal—truly crave.

Lesley needed Lois's calm and contemplative presence, as 1982 was promising to be an active year for the thirty-five-year-old singer, who appeared to be bouncing back from a long and listless lull in her career. Lesley's nomination and appearance at the 53rd Academy Award telecast brought her fresh attention from unlikely outlets. The producers of ABC's wildly popular daytime soap opera, *All My Children*, approached her to compose a tune for their program. The reps behind the show were hoping to score their own spin-off hit record with the acclaimed songwriter from the cultural zeitgeist that *Fame* had become. The end result was "Easy to Say, Hard to Do," which she wrote with Sid Ramin, the genius composer behind *West Side Story* and a long list of notable stage productions and television shows. To further capitalize on Gore's connection to the show, the staff writers wove her into the storyline, where she played music publisher June Gordon. Lesley was also given her own opportunity to sing her original song on one of the six episodes in which she was featured.

While the TV guest spots were fun and encouraging, Lesley was provided the best offer of all by CBS Records—to step back into the private, safe confines of the recording studio.

# HERE SHE COMES AGAIN

With the dual failures of *Someplace Else Now* and *Love Me by Name* never far off the radar, the prospect of a new album came with no small anxiety. There was always the chance that the newfound recognition from the *Fame* franchise, combined with a welcome return from older fans, could make a new album a modest success. Or perhaps the singer's expectations weren't high for a major comeback when she discovered that her next album was to be released on a CBS subsidiary, 51 West, which produced and distributed albums for grocery stores. The small label was proving lucrative for its parent company; by releasing "best of" compilations of the bigger label's catalogue of stars, or recording an inexpensive one-shot deal with an established performer, CBS saw comfortable returns on a relatively cheap investment. By providing minimal, yet capable, session musicians to provide the expansive-sounding backing tracks on new albums, 51 West hit its stride manufacturing low-cost/high-gloss records. Still, Lesley gamely accepted the offer and recorded ten songs, all of them covers of past and current hits by other artists, which could not have allowed for the release of a single, another money-saving move on the part of CBS. Released in May 1982, *The Canvas Can Do Miracles* became Lesley Gore's tenth complete album.

Though the record's most glaring disappointment is the lack of original material, Lesley's interpretations of the selected tracks—chosen, most likely, to create immediate recognition of the song titles for a casual shopper glancing at the back of the album—are worthy of a listen.

Gore both honors and places herself among the pantheon of her generation's female singers and songwriters by covering Carole King's "It's Too Late," Carly Simon's "Haven't Got Time for the Pain," and Dolly Parton's "Here You Come Again." Also among the record's mellow tracks are renditions of Elton John's "Daniel," Boz Scaggs's "We're All Alone," the Bee Gees' "To Love Somebody," and Christopher Cross's "Sailing." Gore's versions of '60s classics—"Chapel of Love" by the Dixie Cups and Jackie Wilson's "Higher and Higher"—provide more upbeat, sparkier breaks from the album's overall lethargic mood. The singer also winks at her reverence for stage musicals by covering "You're the One That I Want" from *Grease*, where she alters a few of the lyrics for gender anonymity—instead of singing she "needs a man," Gore contends that she "needs a friend."

The public simply saw Lesley's name on the cover, smiled at the touch of warm familiarity brought by memories of "It's My Party" and "Judy's Turn to Cry," and went about checking off their supermarket shopping lists; but dogged fans scooped up the record and rejoiced in hearing from an old friend. *The Canvas Can Do Miracles* also boasts one of Gore's best album covers: Lesley's youthful face, still appearing teenaged despite being only a few feet from forty years old, is sketched out in colored pencils, the lines left frayed and incomplete, a work in progress like the artist herself.

But the album's true appeal was the singer's "new" sound—a lower, deeper, natural register, as Quincy Jones usually made her sing an octave higher than her comfortable range to give her that trademark signature "young" sound on her '60s singles. On *Canvas*, the backing tracks sound exactly like the original songs she is

---

**TOP 10 SINGLES MAY 1982***

#1  Ebony and Ivory
    Paul McCartney &
    Stevie Wonder
#2  Don't Talk to Strangers
    Rick Springfield
#3  867-5309 / Jenny
    Tommy Tutone
#4  I've Never Been to Me
    Charlene
#5  Chariots of Fire
    Vangelis
#6  '65 Love Affair
    Paul Davis
#7  I Love Rock 'n' Roll
    Joan Jett &
    The Blackhearts
#8  The Other Woman
    Ray Parker Jr.
#9  Did It In a Minute
    Hall & Oates
#10 Freeze Frame
    J. Geils Band

*From Dave McAleer's *Book of Hit Singles*

covering, putting the sole responsibility on Lesley's voice to make these well-known and established songs uniquely hers. She seems to embrace her age and croons within the organic limitations of her voice, delving into bass-y lows (check out the depressing refrains in "Haven't Got Time for the Pain," almost as though a heartbroken Gore is singing through clenched teeth), intimate, mouth-on-the-mic serenades ("Sailing"), and bounding into surprising, crisp highs (her stellar performance of "Daniel" is as sculpted and meticulous as a luxurious wedding cake). Her delivery is both warm and cool, exorbitant and restrained.

*Canvas*, unlike *Someplace Else Now* or *Love Me by Name*, never promised high hopes of a major musical comeback, which had to have helped minimize any disillusionment that came with the album's quiet release and even softer passing (although it did earn her an invitation to record the bouncy theme song, "My Wildest Dreams," which played over the opening credits to a 1983 after-school special movie, *It's No Crush, I'm in Love*, starring Cynthia Nixon as a student obsessed with her English teacher). Something bigger, something generating a lot more excitement, would soon surface on the blue horizon—Lesley Gore's first radio single in nearly ten years.

# LIGHTNING STRIKES

What would a homecoming princess like Lesley Gore possibly have in common with a swarthy rogue like Lou Christie? Why would anyone pair Lesley, the virginal girl who sobbed her boy troubles into a tear-stained diary, with Lou, the lout beneath the orange glow of a corner streetlamp, wailing throbbing, almost sexual falsettos into the night sky?

Lou, like Lesley, was born to working-class parents on the East Coast, where he would, as a teenager, release a stack of singles that would propel him through a *blitzkrieg* of hits during the '60s. One of the leering sex symbols of his decade, he was born Luigi Alfredo Giovanni Sacco on February 19, 1943, and raised in the suburbs within the tar and cement bustling city of Pittsburgh, Pennsylvania.

And like Gore, Christie showed early fascination with music, and, just as sixteen-year-old Lesley's musical aspirations were guided and nurtured by the older and knowledgeable Quincy Jones, fifteen-year-old Luigi's quest to create music was aided by Twyla Herbert, a classically trained pianist twenty-two years the boy's senior. A flamboyant character with volcanic red hair and a fascination with the occult (Twyla herself claimed to be a clairvoyant, a mystical talent passed down through her gypsy heritage), Herbert's presence can be felt in Christie's first national hit single, "The Gypsy Cried," which soared to #24.

Both singers met as their stars were on their first celestial rise, and each respected the other's work; Gore admired Christie's radically different reggae smash "Two Haves Have I," while he was a fan of her "Look of Love" single. Similarly, both idols were vilified by moral watchdog groups—Gore for her weak character, and Christie, as *TIME* walloped him, for "corrupting the youth" with his implicit sexuality.

Both artists had their singing careers disrupted; Gore went to college, and Sacco served in the military. Both were able to return from their respective hiatuses with substantial hits, despite the soupy British fog in which each tried to revitalize their careers—Lesley's "California Nights," and Lou's #1 smash, "Lightning Strikes" (and the Beatles would go on to cite both of these singers as their American idols).

And both performers struggled with their projected identities, the fictional Lesley and Lou that sold records and teen magazines. Executives tried to change Gore's name before "It's My Party" could do real damage; Sacco wanted to adopt "Lugee" as a one-name moniker, but C&C records credited his first hit to Lou Christie—a stage name that he despised for decades. Lesley's polished, boy-victimized schoolgirl image was in stark contrast to the young woman writhing for individuality and the freedom to love whom-ever she pleased; Lou, with his shirts unbuttoned down his chest, pouty bottom lip and bedroom eyes, was promoted as a doo-wop hoodlum, a bad-boy image that surely denigrated the thoughtful, talented songwriter he actually was. Gore battled criticism for her songs' wimpy, often demoralizing presentation of girlhood; Christie fought constant, belittling comparisons to fellow falsetto front man, Frankie Valli.

Christie and Gore struggled to break free of their bubblegum trappings with more adult fare: Christie's 1971 concept album, *Paint America Love*, was considered his finest work, but failed to generate interest; Gore's masterpiece *Someplace Else Now* would meet the same fate less than a year later. Gore's mid-'70s single "Sometimes" raised hopes of a substantial comeback, then evaporated; Lou's 1974 "Beyond The Blue Horizon" was too pop for the country fans, and too country for the pop crowd, so the single stalled at the bottom of the confused charts, then rode off...well, into the horizon. During the remainder of the decade, Gore kept herself busy with various projects when crowds stopped appearing; Christie also vanished from the scene to pursue interests as varied as oil drilling and hustling rubes as a carnival barker.

And, at one time, both Christie and Gore were managed by Dick Fox, which could explain why the duo ended up on similar oldies touring packages in the '80s, where the unlikely pair would perform duets on stage to rousing, excited ovations. Christie had enjoyed another visit on the American charts with his "Summer '81" medley of Beach Boys tunes, which peaked, coincidentally, at #81. The couple's onstage chemistry (enhanced by what had become a warm friendship) led to a seemingly inevitable Gore-Christie creative endeavor.

The '80s is often remembered, and rightly so, for its "bigness"—big hair, big shoulders, and big wealth. The glamour and largesse of the decade sparkle in TV time capsules like *Dynasty* and *Dallas*; in films like *Wall Street*, *Ruthless People*, and *Brewster's Millions*; and in power rock songs like Foreigner's "I Want to Know What Love Is" and Cinderella's "Nobody's Fool"—all of which dominated the public imagination in 1985 and 1986. Former '60s female acts like Tina Turner and Cher, as well as used-to-be-idols Roy Orbison and the original Beach Boys, had, or were on the verge of, making tremendous commercial comebacks by adopting the bigger, brasher sounds of synth-pop and power ballads that were coming into vogue during the era when Krystle and Alexis Carrington slapped each other into a fountain—and into '80s pop folklore.

It seemed like the perfect time for Lesley and Lou to pool their talents, tease up their hair, don *Miami Vice* shoulder pads, and try for a hit single. Producer Benjy King of Manhattan Records—an offshoot of Capitol Records that had enjoyed a successful relationship with quirky artists like Grace Jones ("Slave to the Rhythm") and Baltimora ("Tarzan Boy")—worked with the pair to release "Since I Don't Have You / It's Only Make Believe," a medley of Skyliners and Conway Twitty '50s torch songs. The 45 was backed with "Our Love Was Meant to Be," which Gore wrote with Lou Christie and Twyla Herbert.

What the record lacks in restraint, it more than makes up for in a list of '80s musical flair and decadent embellishments—trilling electric pianos, synthesized bass, grinding electric guitars, all soaked in reverb for a massive, glittery, luxurious wall of sound. Christie's crying falsetto is smooth, Lesley's vocals are gentle but commanding, and together, howling sharp, dramatic harmonies, they sound exactly as they did in the early '60s. For all its modern 1986 trimmings, Gore's tender performance, backed by Christie's tenor—wafting ghostlike and tuning fork–perfect behind her—can't help but elicit romantic Golden Age memories of warm August nights on the main drag, of slow dancing at the junior prom, of sharing a milkshake along the boardwalk midway.

Its flip, "Our Love Was Meant to Be," is a spunky ABBA-style love song about two people who seem like an unlikely pair (much like the singers themselves) forging ahead, passionate for each other. The song boasts a remarkable blend of Gore's and Christie's voices, so finely tuned with one another that at times it's difficult to separate their vocals. And, like skinny ties and leg warmers, that other '80s mainstay—the smoky saxophone solo—makes its off-putting appearance.

Released in May to capitalize on the romance inherent in long summertime evenings and lakeside first kisses—just the perfect time for a rehashed, cotton candy love song—the single received little airplay, quickly becoming a kitschy novelty record within both singers' catalogues. Radio programmers shrugged at the teaming of two of early rock's heroes and failed to wax nostalgic about oldies-but-goodies. The disc was lost in favor of fresher, more cynical acts like Prince, Culture Club, and the Pet Shop Boys.

The unique single didn't ignite pop radio the way it could have (or deserved to), but the decade would not end with a whimper for Gore. In 1989, twenty-six years after "It's My Party" first struck gold, Mercury finally forgave her decades-old debt and paid the singer the balance for her share of the twenty-five million records sold that bore her name (in a juicy twist of fate, the same year saw the recording of Gore's spunky and assured self-reflective song, "America's Sweetheart").

This was an astonishing and tangible victory for Lesley Gore, but the dawn of the '90s would surprise the singer again with something more abstract, more precious, more electrifying than a lightning strike: Validation.

# Part Three

# EVER SINCE

# LESLEYMANIA REVIVED

There is a scene in John Waters's 1988 film *Hairspray* in which "pleasantly plump" teenager Tracy Turnblad (Ricki Lake) and two other nervous young ladies are trying out to become a Council Member on Baltimore's biggest local afternoon dance program, *The Corny Collins Show*. Following a dance-off to the Dovells' "Do the New Continental," the Council grills the auditioning candidates with questions like, "Can you relate to Lesley Gore's records?" Later in the movie, when host Corny Collins spins a slow dance record, the familiar strains of "You Don't Own Me" fill the television studio.

Forget that Lesley Gore didn't appear on any charts with "It's My Party" until a year *after* the story in *Hairspray* takes place, or that "You Don't Own Me" was still two years away from vinyl; Waters's invocation of Lesley Gore was twofold—first, it reacquainted audiences with her music, and second, affirmed how heavy Gore's presence really was in early '60s popular culture, her dominance on the musical scene. In the album liner notes for the soundtrack of *Hairspray*, Waters honors his favorite music and "the boys who got high on cough medicine, the girls with giant hairdos and mosquito bites on their ankles [ ... ] the teens we secretly wanted to be." His appreciation for '50s and '60s Americana would reveal itself in his films' musical selections (*Cry Baby*), in homages to archetypal June Cleaver-Lucy Ricardo characters (*Serial Mom*), or in lampoons of comfortable, conservative social climates (*A Dirty Shame*); but none match *Hairspray*'s giddy, dizzying celebration of Golden Era rock, with its emphasis on "hairhopper" Lesley Gore, her spirit in the film invisible but weighty.

Toward the mid- and late-'80s, records from twenty years earlier were being dusted off and admired with fresh ears. Thanks to TV shows and movie soundtracks, songs once raging on AM radios and now confined to local oldies stations were given new life. Out was in, and the old was suddenly new again; songs "Higher and Higher" by Jackie Wilson, "Iko Iko" by the Dixie Cups, "And Then He Kissed Me" by the Crystals, "Unchained Melody" by the Righteous Brothers, and "Twist and Shout" by the Beatles were resurrected and allowed another run for the sun (and in a few cases, a brief reunion with the American pop charts) in major motion pictures like *Ghostbusters 2*, *Rain Man*, *Adventures in Babysitting*, *Ghost*, and *Ferris Bueller's Day Off*, for just a few honorable mentions.

Gore's indelible hits were ripe for the picking. In a 1983 episode of the animated series *Alvin and The Chipmunks*, Alvin defeats Brittany (one of the Chipettes) in a school election after Brittany's sister, Janette, casts the deciding vote against her, prompting Brittany to cry herself into a version of "It's My Party." The song in its original form surfaces in 1990's *Problem Child*, during a scene in which a snotty little girl throws a tantrum at her party as she watches the little boy of the movie's title throw all of her presents into a swimming pool. It spins again in Cher's 1990 movie *Mermaids*, and throughout the early '90s, "It's My Party" makes at least three television appearances on *Designing Women*, *Beverly Hills 90210*, and *Cybill*. In 1989, a production company, keeping up with entertainment trends established by MTV, filmed the classic song's first official "video." The short is introduced by Gore herself, who plays a nervous news anchor reporting on female terrorists clad in leather miniskirts and high heels, who "crash random parties around the world, stealing hearts, class rings, abducting young men, and leaving an ever-growing trail of depression, tears, and hysterical teenage girls." The rest of the video takes viewers across several continents as Judys steal Johnnys from birthday parties in America, Germany, Japan, Russia, and even a rockin' igloo in the Arctic!

In a 1993 episode of *The Simpsons*, matriarch Marge Simpson and a gal pal blast "Sunshine, Lollipops, and Rainbows" in their stolen car as they lead Springfield police on a high-speed pursuit, *Thelma and Louise* style. Police Chief Wiggum declares the song "appropriate police chase music."

At the tail end of the decade, Lesley Gore appeared with Fabian and Chubby Checker on an episode of *Murphy Brown* to sing their hits and celebrate the fictional journalist's fiftieth birthday. After several years of low-key appearances, Gore was suddenly all the groove.

Among oldies collectors, Bear Family Records is a holy grail. The German-based company releases the most complete packages of artists' recordings, and reissues lost or forgotten albums in CD format. In 1994, Bear reached into the catacombs and assembled a discography of every existing track Lesley Gore recorded for Mercury between 1963 and 1969, including rare demos, alternate takes, foreign recordings, and album tracks. But the greatest find buried within the collection were the ten songs that would have comprised the *Magic Colors* album, heard for the first time since they were recorded and locked away twenty-seven years before. Bear's *It's My Party* anthology remains the definitive treasure trove of Gore's work, and one of the best and most sought-after box sets of a '60s pop act.

It wasn't just her music that was in demand—venues wanted to see the artist herself. When she wasn't skimming the globe, singing to audiences down under in Australia, or on stages in exotic locales like Japan, Italy, and the Netherlands, she became a major draw back home in Manhattan, immersing herself in one engagement after another. By 1994, she began appearing regularly at the elegant Rainbow Room in New York, the exclusive cabaret theater that stretched its art deco spire into the starry night atop the Rockefeller Center. Gore's perfected new act featured a small backing orchestra and allowed her to be close to her audience, to connect intimately with the crowds that filled the booths and banquettes to capacity each night of her stay at the Room. The platform allowed her to nip from a bevy of musical styles, from the jazz she adored, to standards, to Tin Pan Alley, to contemporary songs, as well as a generous helping of the Mercury hits that made her a star.

Several longtime friends appeared in the audience to see Gore in action, including former producer Quincy Jones. Following her show, Jones leapt up on stage and wrapped his arms around her, lifting her into the air; the crowd erupted in cheers and gave the pair of chums a standing ovation.

The Rainbow Room has since become a New York City legend, having shut its doors in 1998 after only a decade of being the place to be, where cool went to be seen and sip on a cocktail. But Lesley Gore got to participate in its brief, enigmatic lifespan, featuring among its many distinguished guests Tony Bennett and Rosemary Clooney. Though the cabaret could not turn enough of a profit to stay in business, it existed—during its initial run—as a sparkling vestige of New York glamour and metropolitan lifestyle.

While Gore appreciated the return of her old fans and the influx of new ones, she had earned the unwanted attention of another stalker. Unlike the attack in the '60s, this was no stranger, but a songwriter she knew and had worked with—someone she had opened herself up enough to trust. She spent 1994 in fear of her obsessed pursuer, and found not just her own safety in danger, but Lois's as well. "The fears begin to mount," Gore told *Biography*. "You begin to fear you're going to have to deal with someone on the street, every time you pick up the phone. This guy was calling me, at one point, eighty times a day."

Police intervened as best they could, issuing restraining orders and curbing the man's constant phone calls with threats of jail time. The stalker's presence slithered and coiled through every part of the singer's life like a serpent, and while the terror at times was consuming, Gore, ever the tireless artist, was able to fashion the experience into a constructive project, a cathartic release of creativity against the razor bite of reality. She began to write about the nightmare, setting her dramatic plight to music, the story unfolding within the confines of a recording studio. "It's a little bizarre," she said of her burgeoning idea to a writer from *Playbill*. "I've dramatized [the stalking situation], and what it did to me and how it affected my life, and [affected me] musically."

After two excruciating years, the threat of the stalker was gone and life for Lesley and Lois fell back into its normal, comfortable routine. But by the mid-'90s, the silver screen, again, demanded Lesley's golden touch.

# ARSENIC AND BUTTERED POPCORN

Three middle-aged women, who were sister-friends in college but separated over time due to busy schedules and the rigorous demands of life, have reconvened at the funeral of another woman who used to be part of what once was their close circle of girlfriends. She had committed suicide, throwing herself from her penthouse balcony following the barrage of sleazy tabloid articles chronicling the dirty details of her husband's torrid affair with a younger woman. The three surviving ladies, reunited in support of their fallen friend, have their friendship galvanized further when each discovers her husband's adultery with younger girls or trusted associates. They help one another engineer each ex-husband's exposure, humiliation, and downfall, then pool their talents into a revenge-for-hire business venture that becomes *The First Wives Club*. Based on the novel by Olivia Goldsmith, the 1996 film was an instant hit with audiences and quickly became one of the top-grossing movies of the year.

Part of the quirky comedy's appeal was certainly its lead actors; Goldie Hawn, Bette Midler, and Diane Keaton saw their careers rejuvenated, and each earned great sympathy (and laughs) as the scorned ex-wives skewered their philandering men. Besides the biting, satirical script, the movie was set to the pulse of a great soundtrack featuring '60s songs like "A Beautiful Morning" by the Rascals and "Think" by Aretha Franklin—the records that bound the younger schoolgirls together. But one of the movie's finest highlights is in its closing moments. When the three women reminisce once more about the friend they lost, they are reminded of the one record that they memorized, danced to, loved: Lesley Gore's "You Don't Own Me." Midler, Keaton, and Hawn erupt into their own version of the song, and audiences left the theaters, empty popcorn cartons in hand, humming the familiar tune.

Gore was thrilled that "You Don't Own Me" forced its way back into the spotlight, standing defiantly with arms akimbo. With *The First Wives Club* a top draw across the nation, Lesley, back in New York, would haunt the sidewalks outside the theater nearest her home, watching and listening to the enthusiastic crowds as they spilled out of the lobby singing slightly off-key with all their hearts, "Don't tell me what to say! Don't tell me what to do!"

Lesley's next visit to the movies would not be as joyful observer, but as contentious participant. Director-screenwriter Allison Anders had conceived a film chronicling a decade in the life of fictional Edna Buxton (who adopts the more aesthetic *nom de plume*, Denise Waverly, as her career ignites) and the ten years she spends writing hits for artists out of the Brill Building in its early '60s heyday. In a fit of creative epiphany, Anders scribbled down on a hotel napkin the enticing gimmick of the film—to unite original Brill Building songwriters and performers with modern artists, a fusing of old and new, to create the '60s-sounding soundtrack. The project was greenlit immediately, and the crew worked fast to contact the retired Brill apostles, and track down current singers who would embody fictional oldies acts (Madonna made the initial list, but ultimately did not participate).

*Grace of My Heart* concocts characters pieced together from a mosaic of Golden Era idols. Denise Waverly (Illeana Douglas) is based on Carole King, a songwriter who struggles to find her own voice while sending others to the top of the music charts. She marries Howard Caszatt (Eric Stoltz), and together—like real-life counterparts Carole King and Gerry Goffin—they compose hit records for a stable of stars produced by their boss, Phil Spector–lookalike Joel Milner (John Turturro). The movie offers a mélange of treats for oldies aficionados who can recognize the songs and artists being remembered and lovingly homaged: The fictional girl group, the Luminaries, are a combination of the Dixie Cups and the Supremes; the Luminaries' biggest "hits" are "Born to Love That Boy" (reminiscent of any of the

Chiffons' odes to extreme devotion), a wedding song called "I Do" (a "Chapel of Love" copycat), and the scandalous "Unwanted Number," about a child born out of wedlock in the black ghettos (like "Love Child," by the Supremes). The Williams Brothers deliver an uncanny impersonation of the Everly Brothers in "Love Doesn't Ever Fail Us." Jill Sobule channels her best Skeeter Davis impersonation for the Nashville-flavored "Truth Is You Lied." Tiffany Anders and Boyd Rice perform "Absence Makes the Heart Grow Fonder" in a style that recalls Paul and Paula. "Groovin' On You" conjures up the late-'60s Shangri-Las. A doo-wop ballad, "In Another World," suggests the Flamingos and their slick, so-romantic-it-hurts cover of "I Only Have Eyes For You." Matt Dillon plays Jay Phillips, the manic, brilliant-but-tortured leader of a surf band based on Brian Wilson and his Beach Boys. And later in the film, Joel Milner produces a rich, dramatic single for Denise Waverly, which promptly flops, the disappointment triggering Milner to leave the business entirely; this set piece echoes Spector's near-retirement from the music industry after Tina Turner's mesmerizing, powder-keg masterpiece "River Deep, Mountain High" failed to resonate with listeners.

One of the film's best moments (which leads to one of the soundtrack's strongest tracks) comes when Denise has been assigned to write a song with fellow songwriter Cheryl Steed (Patsy Kensit), with whom Denise shares a tense, subtly antagonistic relationship. The women eventually bond when they meet Kelly Porter (Bridget Fonda), a pop princess with an angelic image and an unflappable Jackie Kennedy flip hairdo. The songwriters cozy up to the ingénue to get a sense of who she is as a person, and pick up on the nuances that suggest her friendship with her female roommate is more involved than what first appears. Denise and Cheryl write "My Secret Love," about two people who must conceal their desires lest they face abuse; the narrator swears she'd "rather die than tell" the truth behind their passion.

Lesley, clearly the model for the preened Kelly Porter, was approached to help compose a song that the closeted lesbian character could safely get away with on 1963 radio; the filmmakers were hoping that going straight to the former pop princess herself would give the fake oldie track the authentic Lesley Gore sound. From the beginning, the relationship between Lesley and the movie's music supervisors was far from graceful.

Gore explained in a 2005 interview with Shauna Swartz, "They called me up to write one of the songs, and I felt good that they called me, and then the next thing I knew, I received a song in the mail written by [David Baerwald and music producer Larry Klein], and I was so disappointed that I wasn't brought in on the ground level." Still, she took what was given to her and "doctored" the lyrics, editing the misused grammar and revising the clunky rhymes—"real pet peeves of mine," she said. The end result still seemed to her contrived, not something she totally wanted to be associated with, "until I put in a few lyrics that meant something to me," she explained, "then I felt, well, at least I can put my name on it."

Her detachment to the song may also stem from the producers' treatment of Lesley after her work on the song was finished. She was given a third writer's credit for her contributions to the tune, but perhaps because the fixes and repairs she made to the original draft unintentionally offended or bruised the egos of the other songwriters whose work she attempted to personalize and improve (which ultimately made it a stronger song for the Kelly Porter character), Gore was left out of the festivities that went with the film's debut. She felt more than a little taken advantage of that she wasn't asked to stroll down the red carpet even after they had added her pedigree name to the impressive list of contributors to the film's score. "They had the nerve never to invite me to the opening when it premiered in New York," she said. "So I say fuck them."

Despite the open hostility and smarting sense of being exploited that working on *Grace of My Heart* left in its rubble, "My Secret Love" is nevertheless a stunning song that could have found a happy home on any of Lesley Gore's early albums. Sounding a lot like "You Don't Own Me" in meter and melody, the verses—undulating in an ominous minor key—describe the secrecy, the shadows, the deceit necessary in keeping the characters' clandestine love affair alive. The chorus, where the narrator pledges to keep their romance a secret, vowing to sacrifice her life before exposing her partner to the slings and arrows of injustice and hatred, explodes in a full, dramatic major key that ends in a musical orgy of trilling flutes, bleeding saxophone, and weeping strings. The delivery by singer Lily Banquette is riveting—she is able to convey yearning, strength, and the unmistakable sense of defeat, articulating and humanizing the fictional Kelly Porter's aching love against the terror of being discovered.

"My Secret Love" may not have represented one of Gore's happiest hours, but it's one of the best songs from the movie, a distinct Lesley Gore tune in style and message, one that fans then and now easily connect and identify with, to add to "mix tapes" for their secret girlfriends or boyfriends.

Of any grudges that may have festered from the dysfunctional collaboration on *Grace of My Heart*, Gore claimed to have outgrown them. In fact, 1996 gave her little time to rest. Besides having her music appear in two significant films, she was asked to lend her voice to a concept album of songs from the stage musical, *The Life*, which follows hard, gritty characters slinking along the gutters of New York City in the '70s before the city underwent its family-friendly transformation as a tourist mecca. The roster of singers on the album—including the indomitable Liza Minelli, Lou Rawls, and ninety-nine-year-old George Burns (!)—is as eclectic as the seedy characters in the original musical.

Lesley, sporting her full feminist armor, helmed the song, "My Body," which condemns anyone who might objectify, vandalize, and attempt to dominate women's bodies through legislature or brute force. While Lesley's voice possesses an inherent warmth, a certain level of compassion in even the saddest songs, "My Body" is unique for its complete and utter lack of friendliness, its redaction of Gore's typical infusion of cordiality. Her voice, low and raspy, is purely on the offense, calling the bluff of any man who dares to cross her in the nutcracker of a track.

In 1998, Gore would soften her vocals to participate in another celebration of Broadway show tunes when Richard Loos, president of Rhino Records, had the idea to invite oldies artists together and record songs from *Grease* in a style that would sound truer to the Golden Era sound. Loos had been frustrated with the 1978 movie soundtrack, writing that "when the first single, 'You're the One That I Want,' was released, my joy turned to heartbreak. The song was about 2 percent '50s and 98 percent pop/disco." For him, the remainder of the album "was not significantly better," and sought to answer his own rhetorical question—"Ever wonder what the music from *Grease* would have sounded like if it had actually been recorded in the '50s by '50s recording stars?" For this project, Lesley was reunited with Lou Christie, along with early rocker Freddy "Boom Boom" Cannon ("Tallahassee Lassie") and girl-group legend, Darlene Love ("He's a Rebel").

The completed album, *Grease Is the Word: Boppin' Tunes from the Hit Movie*, admirably pulls off the feat of sounding not like a concept album, but of a genuine oldies compilation of hits, thanks to the musical arrangements (produced, in part, by Loos himself) that restore the four stars to their former teenage, angsty youth: Darlene's version of "Hopelessly Devoted to You" sounds like Spector's "Be My Baby"; Lou delivers a surf-style "Grease," and croons luscious ballads with a haunting, eerie beauty in tracks like "Those Magic Changes" and "Sandy"; and Lesley's line-up is terrific—"Look at Me, I'm Sandra Dee" borrows the Latin riff from the Diamonds' "Little Darlin'"; "It's Raining on Prom Night" and "Freddy My Love" both sound as if they had been lifted from one of her early Mercury LPs; but her strongest cover is "There Are Worse Things I Could Do," which adopts the distinct flavor of "You Don't Own Me," including a rich backing choir and giant chiming bells. (However, for who is having the most fun, my money is on Freddy Cannon—he still sounds like the kid growling his way through 1959's "Way Down Yonder in New Orleans," and seems to relish, like a teenager, in using the dirty words peppered throughout "Greased Lightnin'.")

After forty years of making music, the '90s would end in one of Lesley Gore's crowning achievements—as well as two of her most devastating losses.

# GIVE MY REGARDS TO BROADWAY

In 1963, the Drifters told us that the neon lights shine brighter on Broadway, that there is a distinct sense of magic in the air—probably a mix of hope, of purpose, and of bitter disappointment. Their #3 hit record, "On Broadway," captured the sparkle of marquee lights, and the debris of shattered dreams, as the polished stages of Broadway make stars out of some, and send the rest home in shame on sputtering Greyhound buses.

The thirteen-mile stretch of boulevard runs north and south, its concrete tongue rolling through Manhattan, the Bronx, and Yonkers, where it ends, appropriately, at the fabled village of Sleepy Hollow. Between the section of Broadway bisected by 42nd and 53rd Streets stand the glowing playhouses and proud, arrogant concert halls that comprise New York's famous Theater District—christened the "Great White Way" at the turn of the twentieth century by journalist Shep Friedman when he was blinded by the terrific galaxy of lights that lit signs and building facades. Someone later would add that every bulb that burns bright on Broadway represents yet another broken heart.

Lesley moved closer to attaining the goal of appearing on Broadway in 1997, when she helped stage a cabaret show at the Guild Hall in East Hampton, New York. Called *When Women Run the World*, the show would feature female artists honoring and celebrating the work and contributions of other influential, inspirational women. One unusual bit of casting included feminist politician Bella Abzug, at the age of 77, in the role of sexy chartreuse Marlene Dietrich. "She does a fabulous imitation of Dietrich," Gore told David Lefkowitz of *Playbill* in 1997. "And she'll wear the cutaway and the top hat. This is something she's done at private parties for friends. I thought it would be fun."

Abzug, the outspoken US representative from New York, was affectionately referred to as "Battling Bella" for good reason—she rose to political power in the '70s during the growth and surge of the Women's Movement, and chaired such organizations as the National Women's Political Caucus and the National Commission on the Observance of International Women's Year, to help advance equality, and civil and corporate rights, to women still struggling to find their own piece of the American dream. Not restricted to the advancement of women, Abzug was also a major voice in the fight against racism, in raising awareness for the health and rights of children, and was an early proponent of gay civil liberties.

Gore had formed a fast friendship with Abzug in the early '80s, a time when a struggling and disenchanted Lesley desperately needed a mentor. The singers she idolized growing up were fantasies, unreachable celestial beings who existed only as voices on records; but Abzug was flesh and blood, a salt-of-the-earth character who was approachable and wise. She was the model that Lesley didn't know she was seeking early on when the singer was still forced to project a false and uncomfortable front in the '60s. Lesley told *Biography*, "I think Bella showed me that freedom for the first time. A fabulous woman, but not a woman who was going to be a nice little girl. Somehow that answered a lot of questions for me, seeing that I could act like Bella, that I could be a strong, powerful woman, and that was all right. That helped me a lot toward independence."

As Gore grew older, Abzug's role as a mentor helped aim the trajectory of the singer's future career and projects. "The work she does for women, her concerns for the environment and breast cancer, it's work I aspire to," Lesley said. "Plus, she'll always take another risk. She's never too old to do so."

The friendship, though, would feel all too brief to Gore. Just eight months after the cabaret in the Hamptons, in March of 1998, Bella Abzug died of complications after enduring a risky open-heart surgery. Lesley was devastated by the loss and never missed an opportunity to discuss her friend's legacy. "The whole community really misses her a lot," she told Shauna Swartz several years later.

"We all get together periodically, and it's Bella we talk about, because she was so dynamic and we miss her so. And there are so few women who can pull women together that way." Gore's humble statement ironically undercut her own unacknowledged ability, throughout most of the '60s, to galvanize young women, to unite them each time one of her two-and-a-half minute teen soap operas blared out of car stereos.

As Lesley reeled from the absence of her friend, she would suffer a more crushing blow just two months later.

On May 21, 1998, Leo Gore died at the age of 79. Keeping with Jewish burial and mourning customs, the services at the gorgeously gothic Riverside Chapel in New York were held the day after he passed.

Leo was the first to record his daughter's voice, the first to introduce her to the arts and encourage her to listen to—not just hear—melody, to the story contained within the sound, to the way the song is rendered, molded, sculpted. He encouraged her career in music, and stayed involved every step of the way during the Mercury years, always protecting her to the best of his abilities. In his autobiography, Morris Diamond remembered Leo with humor: "Being the stage parent that he was, Leo Gore was constantly on the phone with the president of Mercury Records, Irving Green. He was not the usual parent nudge, but wanted to be kept abreast of the progress of Lesley's new hit record." After a while, Irving politely persuaded Leo to direct any further calls to Morris or Quincy. Leo approved his daughter's personal appearances, and when he couldn't accompany her himself, sent Ronny in his place. Meanwhile, Leo would, in return, politely persuade Lesley's handlers that he trusted them (he did, in fact, trust Jones and Diamond, but a dad's watchdog nature cannot be unplugged or rerouted).

"Both of her parents loved and supported her," offered a Gore relative, "but Leo really believed in her music career from the beginning. Ronny was a little more cautious about it all, but Leo's faith in what his daughter could do never wavered."

The loss of Leo's tremendous presence would not be felt more sharply or bittersweet than in 1999, when his daughter appeared in front of the Broadway footlights that had once captivated his little girl, a rapt pupil devouring the music and spectacle of *My Fair Lady*. Lesley was invited to spend a few weeks in July appearing in *Smokey Joe's Café*, a foot-stomping musical celebrating the catalogue of tunes by brilliant, influential rock 'n' roll songwriters Jerry Leiber and Mike Stoller—and rewarding Gore with yet another meteoric career highlight. The rock revue, consisting of song performances with no dramatic filler, wasn't a critical smash, and it was hard finding a contemporary critic who appreciated the effort. But it was wildly popular among audiences, running a record 2,036 performances, and attracted the likes of Gladys Knight, Rick Springfield, Ben E. King, Gloria Gaynor, and Tony Orlando to make guest appearances in its rotating cast. In 1998, *Smokey Joe's* would surprise the somewhat exclusive theater world with its three nominations for a Tony Award (including "Best Musical"), and the cast album would go on to win a Grammy a year later.

Gore didn't allow even a moment of the experience to pass her by unappreciated. "It was the best," she told *Digital Interviews*. "I really tried, because I said to myself, 'This is *Broadway*.'" Boasting a fantastic trove of early jukebox jewels, Lesley joined a large cast of about thirty singers to pay tribute to hits like "Jailhouse Rock," "Kansas City," "Yakety Yak," "Love Potion #9," and the moving "Stand By Me." Performing at the Virginia Theatre on 52nd Street—the venerable old playhouse haunted by past performances of *Our Town*, *Cat on a Hot Tin Roof*, *Annie*, *My Fair Lady*, and even the infamous *Carrie*, based upon the Stephen King horror novel, with music by Michael Gore—Lesley was ecstatic at the team effort, the electric excitement of simply being there. "People come to this show to do their very best and when you get twenty or thirty people on a stage the song becomes greater than the part," she explained to Gina Lance. "I won't soon forget it."

Still coming down from the high of working on *Smokey Joe's Café*, Lesley combined efforts with her brother once more to write for the big screen. This time, the project was the 1999 comedy *Superstar*, detailing the misadventures of a clueless, clumsy girl named Mary Katherine Gallagher, a character made popular by comedienne Molly Shannon during her successful run on *Saturday Night Live*. Mary Katherine, like Coco from *Fame*, yearns to be a star and win the hearts of audiences around the world—or at least at home on the stage of her high school gym.

The Gores were a clever fit for the soundtrack, between the experience of Lesley's teenage stardom and Michael's extensive background in musical theater, which combined provided the essence of what *Superstar* was about. Dreaming of fame (both the status and, evidently, the 1980 musical), Mary Katherine warbles her version of "Out Here on My Own" when she tries out for the school talent show. For the film's theme song, the Gores contributed the delightfully gay-camp electronic dance track, "You Wanna Be a Star (Superstar)," reveling in celebrity, narcissism, and dazzling self-confidence.

The kindest critics were only lukewarm to the movie, but *Superstar* was still one of the better productions to be spawned from the *Saturday Night Live* juggernaut, as the film went on to gross more than double its production costs and develop a cult following thanks to Shannon's quirky, indelible character sketch. Still, Lesley was pleased with her own participation, which proved to be a far happier experience than songwriting for *Grace of My Heart*.

The '90s would end with Lesley singing a Gore-Gloria Nissenson ballad called "We Just Can't Walk Through Life" for President Clinton, followed by one more appearance on CD, this time for a charity project that would channel funding to projects in northern New Jersey. Homespun artists, including Bruce Springsteen, Gloria Gaynor, and Janis Ian, lent their time and talents to the heartwarming album, *Songs for the Soul*, a patriotic celebration of the Garden State. Singing with Michael-Demby Cain and backed by the John Harms Performing Arts School, Lesley recorded "All One Family," a stirring song Gore wrote to cope with the loss and remembrance of friends she lost to the AIDS epidemic.

As the world ushered in New Year's Eve 2000, boldly laughing in the face of the hilariously false, dire predictions that the planet would fall into ruin and despair over a couple of misplaced computer digits, no one could have predicted the catastrophic events just on the horizon, the blistering crack in history that would make everything that happened before September 2001 seem so irrelevant, so innocent, and, sadly, so irretrievable.

# DIRTY DEEDS

The opening lines of the US government's *9/11 Commission Report* are strangely literary, reading like a novel instead of a presentation of statistics and figures by a federal panel: "Tuesday, September 11, 2001, dawned temperate and nearly cloudless in the eastern United States." Though what follows in the rest of the report is mired in controversy, the opening line, at least, presents a resonant, honest snapshot of America that morning—no one, as they dressed for work, rushed through crowded delicatessens ordering quick break- fasts and coffees, or crossed highways, bridges, and tolls to file into Manhattan, was expecting the nightmare that would unleash its horrors on an unsuspecting nation in waves throughout the course of what had started as a typical, innocuous weekday.

As planes careened into skyscrapers, rocketed into national land- marks, and plunged into fields en route to major targets, the country held its collective breath until the worst, for that time, seemed over. Once the smoke and debris cleared, rescue workers tallied up 3,000 victims, including entire police outfits and fire brigades.

The tragedy hit Lesley's home, her heart; the apartment she shared with Lois was only eight miles away from Ground Zero, ordinarily a safe distance between two points, but terrifyingly close considering eyes from around the globe were watching the calamity unfold on live television from frightened, silent distances—and the next jetliner crash was anybody's guess.

That brutal holiday season, Americans sought comfort food any- where they could find it. On TV, comedienne Carol Burnett scored a ratings coup when her cast reunion special aired in November. In movie theaters, *Harry Potter and the Philosopher's Stone*, and six months later, *Spider-Man*, each earned nearly a billion dollars in ticket sales, suggesting that an aching nation craved to escape into a fantasy world, and to be rescued by a homespun superhero. A couple of American idols made unexpected returns to popular radio as listeners sought the finest, purest representations of their patriotism and grief—Whitney Houston's stirring "The Star Spangled Banner" and Elvis Presley's melancholy "America the Beautiful" both rose to #6 in the wake of the attacks.

Lesley enjoyed at least one small distraction from the pall still suffocating a country in shock, when in late 2001, the cable channel A&E premiered an episode of their *Biography* series devoted to the pop singer, which Gore happily praised as "pretty darn good." With the renewed exposure of the A&E special and its concurrent magazine interview, Lesley lent her name to yet another novelty album with an irresistible twist.

Multitalented producer, musician, writer, and artist Cevin Soling enjoyed success with his band, the Neanderthal Spongecake, and their surreal debut album from 1998, *The Side Effects of Napalm*. Rock and college radio loved the record, giving it ample airplay to attract hip fans who celebrated the band's sense of irony and absurdity (the New York natives billed themselves as Czechoslovakian nationals who once led a political resistance movement against Communist leaders—a gag that their fans laughed at well before anyone else seemed to get it). The bizarre and darkly humorous overtones of the tracks brought a few of the titles individual attention: "Tastes Like Chicken" made it to Dr. Demento's comedy radiocast, which helped develop the song's cult status, while "This Thing" and "Buffalo" propelled the band into regional stardom and onto an elite short list of the city's hottest bands.

The album boasted one unusual track that would springboard to still another, broader experiment. Inspired by Eric Clapton's reimagining of "Layla," Soling had persuaded Kevin Dubrow, the troubled singer from the heavy metal band Quiet Riot, to record an acoustic, "unplugged" version of the wild, head-banging anthem, "Metal Health." The stripped down song was rewarded with significant airplay, and the notion of taking something familiar and making it new, almost unrecognizable, intrigued Soling enough to pursue a larger project that would skewer the expectations of music fans and aficionados.

Taking about two years to assemble his stars and collect financial backing, Soling handpicked established performers from across a universe of genres and paired them up with songs that no one would ever expect to hear come out of their golden throats, pulling artists from around the world for the creation of an album that Soling described to this author as "a labor of love and chutzpah." He flew to Honolulu to record Don Ho's version of Peter Gabriel's "Shock the Monkey," and jetted to Hong Kong to feed English lines to Jackie Chan's version of Nat "King" Cole's "Unforgettable" (aided in the duet by the steamy voice of Ani DiFranco, the stuntman delivers a lovely rendition, charmingly thick accent and all). Some of the stronger, more bewildering tracks include the blue-eyed soul '60s band, the Box Tops, covering Blondie's "Call Me"; the Fixx provides a spooky, ethereal cover of Nancy Sinatra's "These Boots Are Made for Walkin'"; and soul-gospel singer Billy Preston tackles Duran Duran's "Girls On Film." Soling even enlisted the aid of his former Neanderthal Spongecake bandmates, who had split up the year before, to record T. Rex's "Get It On (Bang a Gong)."

As executive producer, Soling managed the entire project from start to finish, but, running low on time and interest on the time-devouring project, some of the individual tracks were doled out to other producers to complete. Originally, Soling had conceived of the remake of "Dirty Deeds" to sound as if it had been recorded by teen queen Lesley Gore in 1963, but then AC/DC found the old record, dusted it off, and remixed it with modern trimmings—a detailed backstory more aligned to the sonic contrasts Soling wanted to score with the completed album. Instead, producer Mauro DeSantis went for a fairly straight cover of the song, which still provided a jolt in its own way—pop princess Lesley Gore guns it as she growls and grinds over the revved-up backing track, all pistons greased up and firing.

*When Pigs Fly: Songs You Never Thought You'd Hear* was released in 2002, and to the delighted surprise of Xemu records, who up until then had enjoyed regional success with hometown performers, the album garnered national attention when trade magazines like *Entertainment Weekly* took notice of the quirky project. Melinda Newman of *Billboard* wrote jovially that the record "is a fun album to stump guests with at a party. I figure the more tequila you've had, the funnier this album gets." As hard as compilation records are to sell and easy to bypass, Soling dutifully made the rounds, logging in over forty radio interviews to promote the finished CD. At one point, when Billy Idol heard Peter Noone's very Herman's Hermits-style cover of the raucous "White Wedding," the hard-edged rocker reportedly grinned and said sportingly, "Frightening!"

Following the attacks on the World Trade Center, stage and film stars began a tenacious drive to bring skittish playgoers back into the heart of the city to help rescue a struggling Broadway, which had seen a whopping 80 percent decline in audience attendance. Among the strongest allies, which included stage heroes Matthew Broderick, Nathan Lane, Glenn Close, and Bernadette Peters, was actress Rosie O'Donnell, who started featuring numbers from musicals on her massive hit TV talk show in a bid to entice locals and tourists back onto the streets of Manhattan.

Lesley, both a fan of and participant in musical theater, joined the rally. Gore anchored herself in New York for a while, where she would take a break from extensive touring. "Right now I'm feeling pretty patriotic," she told *Girl Talk*, "[so] I'm trying to stick around the states." Gore turned her unfaltering energy to assisting a local acting and singing company called the 92nd Street Y, where she curated a handful of shows on rock history. "I'm always busy," she said, "even if I'm not on stage performing every night."

Gore also went to work with Michael on another reboot of the *Fame* franchise, and she shared her vision for the possible TV series with a writer from *Digital Interviews*. The Gores' concept was to revisit the school from the original Fame twenty years later and tell fresh stories involving the new teaching staff and incoming students. An enthusiastic Lesley said, "I think we're probably going to have Coco,

Gore appeared as the Pink Pussycat on the campy '60s TV show *Batman*. (ABC/Photofest)

Gore poses with her musical mentor, Quincy Jones. (Echoes/Getty Images)

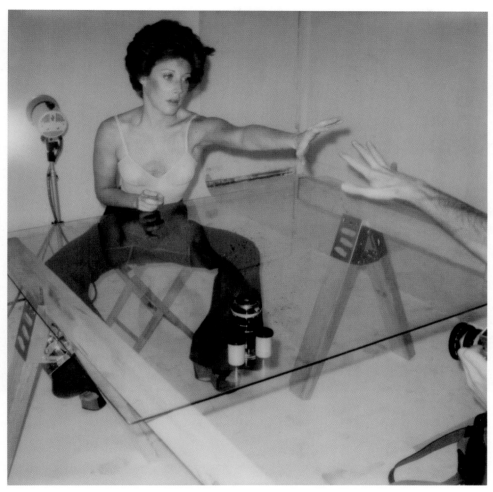

Rare glimpse of Gore posing for the notorious cover of her 1976 album, *Love Me by Name*. (Ginny Winn/Getty Images)

Gore appears on *Sha Na Na*, a '70s musical comedy TV show that celebrated Golden Era idols. (SONY Pictures Television/Photofest)

Golden Era icons Lesley Gore and Chubby Checker appear together in a 1998 episode of *Murphy Brown* to celebrate the fictional journalist's '50s-themed birthday bash. (Time & Life Pictures/Getty Images)

Gore at the opening of her Rainbow and Stars show with her beloved role model, Bella Abzug. (Ron Galella/Getty Images)

A radiant Gore appears at the 2014 Women's Media Awards, just three months before her sudden passing. (Jemal Countess/Getty Images)

Gore enjoys a night out with her partner of over thirty years, Lois Sasson.
(© Jessica Burstein/Corbis)

Irene Cara, come back as a teacher [ . . . ] where she kind of hands over the baton to one of her students." That version never came to fruition, and it appears that neither Gore would ultimately have any connection to the shunned *Fame* series that premiered in the summer of the next year— a failed copy of what rival talent search *American Idol* had perfected.

Lesley turned her attention to a nearby group of performers who were embarking on a project close to the singer's heart, slightly north of Broadway—in Nova Scotia. In mid-2004, the Young Production Company was celebrating five years as an organization dedicated to inviting children and young adults to participate in theatrical opportunities. To honor the anniversary, the troupe staged "My Town, My Guy, and Me," which continues the story between Johnny, Judy, and the fictional Lesley at the botched birthday bash in "It's My Party"—and Lesley, following the example of Bella Abzug, showed up to support the kids.

Artistic director John Brown expressed anxiety over the singer's visit to the set, particularly on the part of seventeen-year-old Erica Achenbach, who portrayed Lesley in front of Lesley. The terrified actress had nothing to worry about; Lesley told a reporter from the *Spectator* that Achenbach's performance was "amazing," and praised how songs that spanned a decade could be unified into one cohesive "wondrous" show.

But Brown had a logistical problem as well. He wrote, "After I had introduced Lesley Gore to the audience and the curtain finale was done, I suddenly thought to myself, 'How do I end this? How do I get Lesley off stage?' You simply can't turn the lights off, walk off in the dark, and this be over." Gore came up with the admirable solution: In front of a surprised and ecstatic audience, she performed a couple of songs with the cast, then took the time to hug, kiss, and praise every actor on the stage. One of Brown's favorite moments from that night was a twelve-year-old performer's facial expression when he received individual attention from the singer. "For me this was intoxicating," Brown said. "My generation's exposure to the Gore material immediately guaranteed that I would have been enamored with Ms. Gore, but a thirteen-year-old boy who had to be educated and deliberately exposed to the Gore material, [his] reaction was exhilarating and a sign that this material will survive to another generation."

After the show, Lesley sliced up five birthday cakes (one for each year of the company's existence), signed hundreds of autographs, and joined the director and the play's three lead actors for a private dinner, offering suggestions and notes for future productions. The show that evening concluded without a single incident gone wrong, and Lesley was able to assuage any nervousness among the director and his cast and crew. Brown praised her professionalism and offered in conclusion that she was "a truly warm and wonderful person."

In 2004, Lesley made the bold, brave choice to host the groundbreaking television series *In the Life* on PBS, which, during its stunning twenty-year run, ran in-depth stories on the lives and struggles of the lesbian, gay, bisexual, transgendered, and questioning community of viewers. Over the years, she had amassed a substantial gay following—the girls viewed Gore as an empowered woman artist, the guys could relate to the boy-fixated tunes, and the community as a whole embraced the elements of irony and coiffed camp in Gore's '60s good-girl front. She exuded something innate that made others feel they could trust her without fear of judgment or criticism, a sense, even in her early records, of being everyone's friend. In one interview, Lesley described an acquaintance of hers who made a painful and potentially humiliating confession to her that he could not share with his own wife and children—that he was a cross-dresser. "It was wonderful to see this change in him," Gore explained to Gina Lance, after the man laid down his burden and began living a more honest life. "I would recommend that for anybody. There is nothing you can be ashamed of. We all have something that we necessarily don't want to tell everybody. But it's okay. It's cool. And you should celebrate who you are."

Hers was exactly the earnest, welcoming attitude that *In the Life* was seeking in its rotating roster of hosts, and the show was the perfect venue for one of the principles that guided the singer's life—to help and inspire young people. Taping the show, she discovered that being gay and out for modern teenagers was certainly easier than it had been for her when she was in high school and college, but there was still a faction of closeted, frightened kids along the conservative, religious bible belt of the American Midwest. Just as teenaged girls reached out to their idol in the early '60s with their relationship woes, gay and lesbian fans flocked to see her when she toured across the predominantly Christian heartland section of the country. Gore was sad but grateful that *In the Life* provided some isolated gay teens their only access to another gay soul.

Though the young female singers crowding today's pop music are forceful and their songs, like Katy Perry's "Roar" or Lady Gaga's "Born This Way," reflect an independence and affirming self-reliance and confidence not present in Golden Era girl songs, modern fans—especially gay men—still gravitated toward Gore's shows; the singer confessed to this author her confusion about seeing seats filled with gay boys and wondered about her appeal to that particular audience—why was a woman in her sixties singing jukebox hits attracting a youthful band of homosexual men? Pop radio's newest stars seem to have forgotten one important tenant about being young: It still sucks being a teenager; it's still soul-crushing to love the one who doesn't realize you're alive; your peers still decide if you're a worthy person, or invisible and disposable. Gore's old records drip with the vulnerability, loneliness, and elusive love curiously absent from the current generation's music, and those old tunes easily sweep up young listeners like a Pied Piper of broken hearts. Even more importantly, today's gay teenagers still can't find in mainstream radio open, young male idols singing songs of love or heartache to or about other boys, so Lesley's timeless message—that boys are mean, but she can't help loving them—resonates deeply with lonely, closeted young men in desperate need of a sympathetic friend.

Lesley's involvement with the TV show was just as much a learning experience for her as well. She explained to *Lesbian News*, "I began to feel comfortable about just coming out and revealing myself—not in a huge way with trumpets and everything else—just in a matter-of-fact way: Here I am; this is where I am and this is what I have been doing and—oh, by the way. . . . "

This process and self-reflection would be instrumental the following year. In 2005, fifty-nine-year-old Lesley Gore would finally reveal her sexuality to the world and live her life fully, truthfully, with no more personal barriers left to kick down—all in the midst of releasing a new critically acclaimed album that would thrust her back into the public's attention.

# BETTER ANGELS

Blake Morgan has known Lesley Gore for most of his life—since he was nine years old, to be precise. Lesley is old friends with Blake's mother, activist Robin Morgan, whose 1970 book, *Sisterhood Is Powerful*, helped drive the American Women's Movement and advance feminist causes. Lesley could recall a time, over twenty-five years before, when the little boy's feet couldn't reach the pedals on his piano.

Since that time, Morgan cultivated his own career in music, first as a stowaway keyboard player (he was too young to appear in many of the clubs where his older friends booked their band's gigs, so they had to sneak their small-statured friend backstage in a drum case), then as a solo artist under Phil Ramone's label, N2K Sony/Red. Performing most of the backing vocals and instruments himself, reviewers from the *New York Times*, *Billboard*, and the music aggregate *All Music Guide* tripped over themselves to praise the renaissance musician's 1997 alternative album, *Anger's Candy*.

Despite the red-hot reception from fans and even adoring critics, Morgan quickly grew wary of the rigid, dogmatic business end of making music—the unyielding, administrative constraints that perpetually conflict with the free flowing, often messy process of making art. Though Morgan had quickly become the label's most successful act, the cynical singer was able to slip through a loophole that let him out of his seven-year contract with Ramone. Like Quincy Jones, Blake Morgan's talents could not be confined to one activity, and his need to create without restrictions spurred him to found his own independent label in 2002, Engine Company Records. With Morgan at the wheel as producer, he and the roster of artists and bands who came aboard ECR were given greater control over their material, and could market directly to consumers with the label's embrace of the Internet and instant access to music.

Morgan approached Gore with the idea of getting her back into a recording studio, doing what she was supposed to be doing all along—making *her* music, on her own terms, instead of being relegated to forgettable cameos on smarmy compilation records like *Happy Holidays Las Vegas* (Tad Hendrickson of the *Jazz Times* claimed the album reeked of "reindeer droppings," and gleefully berated Lesley's cocktail lounge cover of "Christmas in Las Vegas," snickering that it sounded "like an ad put together by the gambling commission [ ... ] So bad it's good? Not even.").

Having paid attention to Gore's previous failed albums, Morgan persuaded her with his conception of the finished product, saying in the *New York Times*, "I think it would be a mistake to make a comeback record. I think it would be a mistake to make a genre record. I think what we need to do is make a great Lesley Gore record." He wisely avoided trying to be trendy and refused to record Lesley in stylish trappings that would ring false with fans, and instead enveloped the singer where she was most comfortable—within the quiet, subtle, intimate setting of a cabaret. The producer shucked brassy and conspicuous backing tracks for an auditory mural that was tender and lulling, with just piano, a gently strumming guitar, and drums caressed by the hushed, sweeping bristles of a brush.

As excited as Lesley always was to introduce fresh material in her shows and audition it to receptive audiences, the twin disappointments of *Someplace Else Now* and *Love Me by Name* were a constant reminder of public rejection, colossal heartache to an artist who infused the best of herself in her work and released it to the world to be accepted or disregarded. But now, pushing sixty, she was living by a new mantra of confronting fears head-on and embracing what might come. As her producer, Morgan promised to work alongside her, not to dominate her, not like in the '70s when Gore was last recording her own songs in a mechanized, tightly controlled industry; those former things had passed away, and this new movement toward unbridled freedom of expression and autonomy were perhaps the biggest incentives. "I think it's fundamentally over," she told Jesse Mayshark of the dying record business. "It's easier to go online."

The carefully selected songs reflect not a woman who has aged, but who has refined, accruing wisdom and experience and grace. Two of the songs are familiar: "Out Here on My Own," which Gore frequently performed live, finally makes an appearance on an album by its creator; and "You Don't Own Me" gets a fresh treatment, its original story centering on a schoolgirl declaring independence from her bully boyfriend having now ripened into an older, more austere relationship.

The title track, "Ever Since," is a perfect introduction to the album, as the phrase literally means "until now from a particular time in the past." The song captures the sense of used-to-be, could-have-been, wish-it-was, an examination of a person that, ever since, has searched and yearned and waited. There comes a chance meeting that finally seems to fulfill the hopes contained in the singer's errant wish upon an eyelash. A line from Mike Errico's beautiful lyrics about the two orbiting characters narrowly avoiding collision lovingly, subtly references Gore's first hit record when she sings about "all the parties I've been to, you were missed."

Songwriter John Fischer contributes "Cool Web," detailing the out-of-control tailspin of a tense, painful relationship that can't seem to keep from imploding on itself. The grim minor keys, punctuated by a throbbing, Spanish-style electric guitar riff, suggests a hot, uncomfortable southwest night, and Gore's delivery of the resentful lyric is both resigned and achingly desperate.

The radio-friendly "It's Gone"—written by Blake Morgan—again touches on Gore's penchant for singing about troubled, tenuous relationships, but this time with a decidedly adult approach. The lyric ponders rhetorically if it's "too much for letting go," "too loud for being heard," "too bright for being seen," a romance that always skirted the extremes and ended in a series of near misses and miscalculations. Morgan continues the album's theme of waiting "ever since" with the song, "Better Angels," where the singer hopes that a miracle will come along and save her, but from what, she's not so sure. "I've been keeping clear of stepping on the cracks," she sings, "I miss just enough to keep me coming back." Though she grieves that "her case looks fatal," she turns the tone of the song by introducing the optimistic, if gravely unrealistic solution for "better angels to come to me"—the vulnerable, sorrowful type of prayer one utters when faith is barely alive, when all other earthbound options are exhausted.

The bold message of "You Don't Own Me" gets a sidekick in Mike Errico's "Someday," a gritty, muddy jazz song set to the relentless heartbeat of a drum and a sinister bass that creates the image of a dark, seedy lounge in a wharf town socked in by fog. "Someday," she vows, "I'm going to get where I'm going," no matter the criticisms of others, the obstacles set before her, or the plastic, phony smiles she must endure from the distrustful figures that haunt her periphery.

Lesley adds some of her own material to the quietly lavish album. "Words We Don't Say," cowritten with Morgan, Errico, Tanya Leah, and Lorraine Ferro, chronicles the breakdown of yet another relationship that ends in regret. The lyrics convey the sense of time wasted and lost, of things not mentioned, of two people who can't meet each other's line of vision. "Trying to hide, night after night," Gore lilts, "drifting away...."

Another standout song is Gore's "Not the First," a track reminiscent of her early '60s tunes, with its plucky beat, double-tracked vocals, music box sound effects, and story of a cheating boyfriend. Speaking from experience (Johnny is not mentioned by name, but his presence is surely felt), Gore sings as one who's seen it all before and anticipates the failures of those who must experience them for themselves: "It's just the same old story," she warns, "but with a difference cast." She tries to warn the victim of the story, to convince her to start thinking with her head instead of her irrational heart, but knows her advice will go unheeded by a willful fool.

The final track is "We Went So High," a previously unrecorded song from the dog-eared Lesley Gore-Ellen Weston notebook.

Whereas "Ever Since" introduces listeners to the lush, elegant, full sound of the backing band, "We Went So High" concludes the record with a simple, devastating voice-and-piano lullaby. The song conjures the image of the tragic Greek figure Icarus, who flew too close to the sun and had his arrogance punished by his tremendous fall to earth. The relationship in "We Went So High" dares the same physical feat, flying so fast "as if we had no weight," flying to such great heights that they carelessly ignore the sensible warning that there is ultimately one place to go, and that's straight down. Keeping with the loss and remorse that feels embedded in the phrase "ever since" (as well as the overall mournful tone of the album itself), Gore is resigned that she'll never experience again the thrill and

| TOP 10 SINGLES JUNE 2005* |
| --- |
| #1 Hollaback Girl<br>Gwen Stefani |
| #2 Don't Phunk with My Heart<br>Black Eyed Peas |
| #3 Behind These Hazel Eyes<br>Kelly Clarkson |
| #4 We Belong Together<br>Mariah Carey |
| #5 Switch<br>Will Smith |
| #6 Incomplete<br>Backstreet Boys |
| #7 Holiday<br>Green Day |
| #8 Lonely<br>Akon |
| #9 Don't Cha<br>Pussycat Dolls |
| #10 Best of You<br>Foo Fighters |
| *From *Billboard* |

passion propelling the brilliant but all-too-brief flight in "We Went So High": they had come so close, she whispers, almost in tears, but "we'll never see it quite so clear" again.

*Ever Since* was released in June 2005, and the response from critics and fans was immediate and gratifying. Mike Joyce of the *Washington Post* praised Gore for the selection of songs and for ignoring the tired trend of recording an assortment of pop standards and Tin Pan Alley relics. "The effort makes her return all the more welcome and enjoyable," he wrote.

The *New York Times* was even more enthusiastic over the new album (Lesley's hometown bought up the first thousand copies in almost no time). Jesse Fox Mayshark wrote a thorough article about the making of *Ever Since*, calling it "as mature and wistful as her early records were brash and bright." Paying Lesley perhaps the greatest compliment she could have hoped for, Mayshark drew comparisons to the singer's musical idols, writing, "Ms. Gore's voice is a little huskier with the years, and her singing shows the influence of the jazz singers she grew up listening to, like Nina Simone and Dinah Washington."

In January 2006, the *Advocate* was even more hyperbolic in its praise. Michael Giltz, in his thoughtful and perky essay, concluded that *Ever Since* "is easily the best album of her career." Joe Viglione of *All Music Guide* concurred, comparing Gore to "a good old friend you haven't seen in years suddenly showing up at the door. It's a welcome return, and hopefully the start of much more music from this creative artist [ . . . ] Just a lovely album quite worthy of your time." Though Lesley's voice had become slightly coarse with age, raspy with the scratches and pops of a vintage vinyl record, that scuffed, tarnished quality adds raw density and weighted meaning to the vocals, which Viglione praised as "exquisitely evolved."

"It was a great record," Phil Ramone told this author. "Blake was a great match for her style. It really emphasized what Lesley was so good at."

Gore's sales enjoyed a further boost when several album cuts were used in TV and film productions. *CSI: Miami* borrowed the bitter "Better Angels" for its fourth season premier, and "Words We Don't Say" made a prominent appearance in an episode of Showtime's lesbian drama, *The L Word*. Director Jeff Lipsky, another New York native, utilized "It's Gone" in his 2006 film about a disintegrating marriage, *Flannel Pajamas*.

Along with the praise being lavished upon *Ever Since*, attention was being turned to the personal life that Gore had lived openly within her own private circles, which she was now sharing (and officially confirming) with the public and with fans. Besides the successful launch of a new album, Lesley was celebrating twenty-five years with Lois.

"This is just an opportunity for me to kind of catch up with myself," Gore told the *Advocate*. Her coming out was a bold move; this was still very much George W. Bush's conservative climate of terrorist alerts, infringement of Americans' privacy, and assaults on civil rights for the LGBT community. Openly discussing her sexuality and longtime relationship with Lois in the July 2006 *Lesbian News*, Gore railed against the president's push for a federal amendment that would deny any and all recognition of same-sex couples. "I think it is the most ridiculous thing I have ever heard," she snapped, "but so typical of his strategy and his thinking."

Lesley and Lois provided a tough picture for the evangelical hard-right to challenge—two hardworking, successful adults who had constructed a happy life bound together by devotion and loyalty that spanned a quarter of a century, especially in a culture where half of all traditional marriages ended in divorce. "Deep down, there is a tremendous amount of love," she revealed to Denise Penn. "I wake up ready to conquer the world every morning because that's sort of the way you need to face New York. And I feel as though I have a partner in that; it is like Lois and myself against the world."

Their two diametrically opposed personalities resulted in a powerful, intense, oftentimes "rowdy" connection that Gore confessed, "certainly isn't dull." Every argument ended with the ladies fighting their way back to each other. Lois—analytical, steady, rational, whose own creativity is focused and solitary—was a strangely perfect match to Lesley's relentless, wild creativity, her daydreamy thought process, her need to share her talents onstage before a crowd in order to find purpose. But even when Lesley hopscotched from state to state on multiple tours, Lois was the steadfast compass in New York, and all roads always pointed to home. The two women were able to keep up with each other's pace, even if the object of the race was not always the same. And Gore contended that it was "just nice to go through life with that kind of companionship."

Younger fans who unearthed her old hits and wanted to check in with the artist today proved to be the largest audience buying up copies of *Ever Since*. Part of the reason for that surprising demographic was that younger generations could better navigate social media with their computers and smart devices, enabling them to easily follow and check in with a performer, keep tabs on their career, and watch for (and download) new releases. Another reason for the appearance of younger fans was that the old teen music, combined with the stormy or forlorn affairs chronicled in *Ever Since*, spoke to twenty-somethings who were dating and breaking up and falling in love again, still maneuvering through the perplexity of young-adult relationships. The up-and-coming generation, too, was far more tolerant of gay people and were neither shocked nor thwarted by a person's sexual identity, placing the deserving emphasis on the merits of the music and not on the personal relationship of the singer. Gore had always hoped that her coming out publicly would help longtime listeners and comfort her closeted fans struggling within the confines of their own fictitious lives, but Gore also couldn't help wondering, and worrying, what her old, first-generation fans thought of her announcement.

There was little time to ponder the question, as the two-year promotion for *Ever Since* took Lesley away from home for touring spurts weeks at a time. Venues were sold out, theaters packed to capacity, and eager crowds waited in long lines to be able to speak with the affable star, who nearly always sat in the lobbies following her performances to spend time with the diverse audiences that came to support and savor her new songs.

*Ever Since* restored Lesley to a place of prominence, with major news outlets and trade journals making space to have a conversation about her current and past accomplishments, a career in constant flux. Other artists clambered to work with her, wanting to feature her voice on their cuts, the addition of a crisply tuned, well-oiled instrument to the symphony. She jammed with the Rock Bottom Remainders, a fun, self-deprecating band composed of such literary heavyweights as Dave Barry, Stephen King, and Amy Tan. She made a guest appearance on Shimmerplanet's "Siren" in 2006, and cowrote the striking piano ballad "Hungry for You," which appeared on the 2008 tribute album, *Hallways: Songs of Carol Hall*. With renewed attention to Gore's discography, Studio Essentials reissued 1982's *The Canvas Can Do Miracles* on CD for the first time in 2009. And in late 2012, again giving her time to assist in a project important to local youth in New York, Gore made a cheeky vocal cameo on a rap song about image and self-respect called "Pull Your Pants Up," written and performed by the children of the Bronx-based public awareness organization, Health People, and its Kids Helping Kids mentoring program. Besides lending her voice to the track, Gore also ensured that the children were given time in a real recording studio so their song had professional polish, and even set them up with a director to help them create a video to generate further interest in, and attention for, a hometown cause.

She often downplayed her philanthropy, wanting only to lend a helping hand or extend a bit of kindness without calling attention to herself with publicity. Fan club president Jack Natoli added that Gore had a knack for finding out if friends or loved ones were experiencing some sort of illness or crisis, and would immediately show up to offer assistance; and more than once, she offered to visit sick fans in their homes or hospitals to sing to them if they needed an up-close-and-personal dose of their hero to cheer them. She even recruited her beloved dog Billie (named after Holiday) in her endeavors, training the pet to become a therapy dog to make hospital rounds and deliver the kind of medication that only an animal can give. Besides being kind to her core, Gore practiced old-fashioned etiquette that endeared her to fans, friends and associates; columnist Liz Smith described the delight of receiving a thank-you note from the singer for some small compliment she paid Gore in a published piece, a polite ritual that seemed to bring Gore great pleasure (a family friend lovingly teased, "She'd send a thank-you note for a thank-you note").

Besides social obligations, Lesley committed herself to a busy work and tour schedule into the 2010s. She continued to headline nostalgia concerts like Bruce Morrow's Palisades Park Reunion, earned her sea legs on special oldies cruises, and made more glamorous appearances at sophisticated dinner club shows like the "Legendary Ladies of Rock" at the Stardust Hotel in Las Vegas (Morris Diamond made the trip to Nevada to see her and was bursting with pride at the audience's reaction). In 2012, Gore participated in the "She's Got the Power" celebration of girlpop at New York's famed Lincoln Center for the Performing Arts, singing beside Spector protégés Lala Brooks and Ronnie Spector. By 2014, Gore was accepting fewer offers to sing, but made time to resurface at events dear to her heart and philosophy. She was a regular face at Broadway premiers and musical exhibitions, and often took the microphone at underground rallies in support of women's reproductive rights; even in the months leading up to her death, Gore was always looking ahead, always diving into her next project. "I'm a musical person," she told the *Advocate*. "That's what I want my life to be about."

Finishing the first decade of the twenty-first century, some fifty years into a career that showed no signs of slowing, Lesley Gore broke ground on two new crowning projects—piecing together her memoirs, and writing a musical with playwright Mark Hampton and composer Debra Barsha about her incredible journey, chronicling the rapid ascent to teen idoldom that could only have happened during rock-pop's fledgling, toddler years in the early '60s. She had a stunning portfolio of work from which to draw—the authentic, thoughtful, mature songs of *Ever Since*; the thumping disco beats of *Love Me by Name*; the wistful portrait of the artist as a young woman in *Someplace Else Now*; the incredible "You Don't Own Me" that roared with defiance in the granite face of socially ingrained sexism and servitude; all leading back to the moment of creation fifty years before—the innocuous seven-inch single on vinyl that consigned a sixteen-year-old American high school junior into rock history with the miscreant Johnny, that tramp Judy, and a party that has belonged to Lesley Gore all along.

Her fans thank her for the invitation to join in.

# START THE PARTY AGAIN

The Taurus, despite its quest for requited, forever-love, and its often bitterly consuming drive for career stability, receives its ultimate sense of peace in authentication, nestling snuggly into its corner of the universe and belonging. Lesley Gore's records have survived for decades, retaining original fans who bopped to the tunes when her records made their first revolutions on Stereophonic turntables (Gore's was one of the longest, continually running fan clubs, since 1963, with its devoted president, Jack Natoli, serving its thousands of international members for an astounding fifty years), and recruiting new fans in each subsequent generation as those crusty fossils are transferred to digital downloads. A testament to the durability of Lesley's music exists in the long list of artists who, enamored by her work, have covered, and cloned, her songs—without the teenager's massive success or earnest charisma. As Oliver Alden wrote in 2001, "Every solo girl after the teen market [ . . . ] took a crack at the Lesley Gore style. Country singers as big as Tammy Wynette showed off her influence. Rock and roll bands told producers that they wanted her sound. Those who needed album filler considered covering her songs. Those who were just starting in the music business copied her. Those who were falling out of popularity tried to inject a touch of her style into their own."

She inspired the very same contemporaries with whom she was competing for chart space in the '60s. The Shangri-Las covered "What's a Girl Supposed to Do," the Cookies elbowed into "The Old Crowd," Reparata and the Delrons borrowed "I Can Tell," the Paris Sisters purred their way through a mawkish cover of "It's My Party," and both Jack Jones and Alvin and the Chipmunks took caramel-apple bites out of "Sunshine, Lollipops, and Rainbows" for their own albums. Ellie Greenwich, who wrote and performed backing vocals for "Maybe I Know," recorded her own version of the song after falling in love with Gore's interpretation. And in those wonderful, bizarre twists of fate that are discovered serendipitously by combing through stacks of CDs, cassettes, and records, Wayne Fontana and the Mindbenders, who shot "A Groovy Kind of Love" to fame when Gore was forced to turn it down, covered her "Off and Running." But the best find is a recording of "I'm Going Out (The Same Way I Came In)" by Helen Shapiro, from whom Gore inadvertently stole "It's My Party" and rode it to the top of multiple music charts.

Several artists also recognized Gore's later work and paid tribute to her brilliant flashes of songwriting from the '70s. Dusty Springfield borrowed "Love Me By Name," and Lesley's composition crossed easily into the rhythm-and-blues arena with emotive, soulful covers by Patti Austin, Jennifer Holliday, and Angie Whitney. Broadway star Bernadette Peters added to the '70s recycling of Gore tunes by recording her own lovely, theatrically dramatic version of "Other Lady."

Of course, Lesley Gore's two biggest hits would attract the most attention from other performers, their remakes clocking in anywhere from respectful cuts to reprehensible rubbish. "It's My Party" would be revamped by no less than ten artists (although Martin Denny would make the odd choice of just covering the sequel, "Judy's Turn to Cry"). In 1973, as Gore was fleeing her sugarplum prison, Bryan Ferry released his own jittery, gender-bending version of "Party." Backed by steel guitars and banjo-picking, country singer Carroll Baker drawled and yodeled her way through a bluegrass remake that somehow managed to climb to #1 in Canada. In 1981, British artists Barbara Gaskin and Dave Stewart unleashed a version so avant-garde and strange that morbidly curious English audiences sent it to the top of England's pop chart. Stateside, Soozy Q blasted a techno dance mix, and R&B singer Brandy sampled "Party's" famous chorus for a rap track (the "cry if I want to" line has been reworked by as incongruent of artists as Robin Thicke, Miley Cyrus, Bret Michaels, and rapper Kitty who rhymes defiantly, "It's my party, couldn't cry if I wanted to."). In 2011, singer Colbie Caillat portrayed Lesley Gore in an episode of NBC's drama *The Playboy Club*, where she performed what stands as the best edition of "It's My Party" after the original.

Even the song's iconic title would be lifted for various projects. Chaka Khan, Cymphonique, Jessie J, and rapper Roscoe Dash all repurposed the title for their own original songs. "It's My Party" would lend its name to a girl-group cover band that records copy-cat versions of girly classics; and in stark contrast to the spunky song that made the title famous, the movie *It's My Party* would tell the story of a gay man who throws himself one final bash to say good-bye to his loved ones before succumbing to complications from AIDS.

In 2010, "It's My Party" was poised to enjoy mainstream success again as a cover by pop singer Amy Winehouse. Winehouse's previous singles paid homage to the Golden Age icons she admired and sought to emulate through her own saloon-and-cigarettes, shabby-glamorous style. "Rehab" begins with the same handclapping riff from "My Boyfriend's Back," and her ballad, "Back to Black," is a Ronettes-style funeral dirge set to a mushed, layered Spectoresque wall of sound (Guy Trebay, the style reporter from *The New York Times*, called Winehouse "a five-foot-three almanac of visual reference," from her Diana Ross beehive, Ronnie Spector Egyptian cat lashes, and her rockabilly Bettie Paige-meets-motor-oil attire). Winehouse loved music she called "jukebox," and several filler songs she recorded—from a reggae version of Sam Cooke's "Cupid" to a stunning, minimal voice-and-guitar cover of "To Know Him Is to Love Him"—displays her respect for the artists and music that ultimately shaped her career.

Following her smashing release of the multi-award winning album *Back to Black*, Winehouse was recruited to contribute a song to *Q: Soul Bossa Nostra*, a tribute album to Quincy Jones. While other artists selected Jones's more complex, soulful sides to cover, Winehouse did not hesitate to select "It's My Party," in honor of the producer's first hit in the '60s, and to acknowledge Lesley's influence on Amy's own metamorphosis. Winehouse decided that the backing track would remain true to the 1963 original; her voice, as rough as the jagged edges of a tin can torn open, would provide the most jarring contrast from Gore's record, giving the plucky tune a tenser, more tragic tone. Jones approved of the track, boasting with pride to *Rolling Stone*, "Amy's talent as an artist is undisputable. I absolutely love what she did to make the song her own."

But Winehouse would not get to enjoy her badly needed comeback or the hit single that may have restored a crippled career that was still so brimming with potential. Like Marilyn Monroe, James Dean, or Montgomery Clift, the young singer boldly, recklessly flirted with catastrophe, and after years of chronic substance abuse, Amy Winehouse died of alcohol poisoning on July 23, 2011. She was only twenty-seven years old.

Like "Party," "You Don't Own Me" took on a life all its own, the song of fierce independence, ironically manipulated and exploited many times over by artists who, loving the original, wanted a chance to try it themselves, like coveting a friend's favorite, envied article of clothing; others simply wanted to claim it as their own, stamping it with their individual, distinctive styles, as if their renditions somehow enhanced and enriched the life of the song like stickers from around the world plastered across an old traveling trunk. It is submitted as conclusive proof that "You Don't Own Me" was, at the time of its release, and ceaselessly since, an important song, an invaluable stitch in America's fabric.

Faithful fan Dusty Springfield delivered a rendition that doesn't waver much, if at all, from the original; she seemed to appreciate what made Lesley's rendition so special, and simply duplicated it note for note (although Springfield's cool, grits-and-gravel voice lends itself to just about anything). And decades later, Bette Midler used the song in her live concerts; herself a Baby Boomer who must have had her pulse on Lesley's music during its '60s heyday, Midler's delivery is bold, forceful, and, true to form, divine.

Those artists who refused to strictly copy the original and forged ahead into certain sacrilege produced renditions that were remarkable for their uncertain, sometimes indefinable loveliness—or for being oddly, shrilly absurd. Joan Jett's version in 1979 doesn't shy away from the rocker's hard edge, but her double-tracked voice and wailing-guitar update of the original background music lends Jett's song a subtle whiff of vulnerability, like flowery perfume that lingers in the air long after the person has left the room. The 1987 soundtrack from *Dirty Dancing* didn't feature Gore's record, but substitutes in her place a seedy, slithery male version from the New Wave group, the Blow Monkeys (although the teasing sexual overtones—a boy declaring his freedom to date other boys—provides perhaps the most memorable twist of all the myriad covers). Rasputina, a Victorian-style strings and vocal group deliciously categorized as "dark cabaret," recorded a macabre, turn-of-the-century boardwalk rendition. In 2010, rap superstar Eminem sampled the line, "You don't own me / Don't try to change me in any way" in his song, "Untitled" (Gore expressed praise for Eminem's visceral lyrics and joked about giving herself the rap moniker "LL Big Puff"). In 2011, Irish-born singer Maxine Linehan released a tougher, punchier cover made distinguishable by the rap performed midway through by the phonetically challenging named Phlaymz. For sheer shock value, give a listen to the 1981 version by German expressionist singer Klaus Nomi, who spits out the verses like a cartoon villain twirling a mustache, then pelts out the chorus in a jolting female operatic trill.

The 2002–2005 NBC series *American Dreams* followed a family and a group of teen friends in the early '60s, with the show's hook being a peek behind the scenes of *American Bandstand*. The gimmick was to have current pop stars perform on the show in the style of '60s artists; Brad Paisley channeled Ricky Nelson, Jennifer Love Hewitt jiggled into character as Nancy Sinatra, and the real-life Duff sisters portrayed the streetwise Shangri-Las. Michelle Branch, whose biggest hit, "All You Wanted," went to #6 in early 2002, materialized as a diminutive Lesley Gore, pelting out a fantastic cover of "You Don't Own Me."

Lesley Gore told *Digital Interviews* of her anthem record, "It's a song that just kind of grows every time you do it. It might mean one thing one year, and *boom*—two years later it can mean something else." This was certainly true in 2012 when "You Don't Own Me" was resurrected yet again during President Barack Obama's second run for the presidency. When Republican nominee Mitt Romney promised to defund Planned Parenthood and demonized other programs and policies crucial to women's health and reproductive rights, Gore, along with Lena Dunham, Alexa Chung, Tavi Gevinson, and Rachel Antonoff, released a public service announcement using the song as fist-shaking indictment percolating in the background as women held up signs of protest. The singer introduces the clip in her gamey, best politico impersonation, "I'm Lesley Gore, and I approve this message."

President Obama would go on to win a second term in office. "That's the kind of thrill that you can't buy," Gore told *Frontier* about her contribution to that season's political showdown. "It's not like selling records. It's not like selling books. It's the influence that the song had on people during a very crucial time. It's not money in my pocket, but it certainly makes my heart swell."

Flipping through the stacks of 45s and LPs, cassettes, CDs, and digital downloads measures not just the rapid, dramatic changes in how music is delivered to fans, but also plots the points of the singer's growth. It is profoundly unfair to dismiss a large body of her work as pure cheese or to oversimplify her early records as vapid "girl group," sweet and disposable as a stick of minty chewing gum. Her '60s singles are rich with nuance: Gore reveals a subtle, prickly sexual jealousy well beyond her age in "It's My Party." She is forced to make the painfully adult decision between sacrifice and self-preservation in "Maybe I Know." She assumes a delightfully lusty guise in "Wonder Boy." Even "Sometimes I Wish I Were a Boy" spits in the eye of convention when Gore flips gender conformity by hoping to become a guy—to ask another guy out. And "You Don't Own Me" remains every generation's battle cry of emancipation, courageously released during a time when shattering institutionalized sexism and misogyny could have ended in career suicide; no one saw the likes of such a tune again until Gloria Gaynor unleashed onto the world (and right into dance clubs) "I Will Survive" in the far more liberated climate of 1979. Gore's entire canon showcases a singer malleable to suit an array of genres and themes; even the briefest survey of albums from *I'll Cry if I Want To* to *Ever Since* is compelling evidence that there is no arrangement or style Gore's voice could not accommodate with relative ease.

Her songs, and the ghost of the teenage pop princess, persist, popping up in unlikely places. In 2001, indie electronic musician Owen Ashworth of Casiotone for the Painfully Alone titled one of his sweet love songs "Lesley Gore on the TAMI Show" in honor of the honey-coated pop princess. And the infectious "Sunshine, Lollipops, and Rainbows" made a delightful, sugar-glazed cameo in 2009's *Cloudy with a Chance of Meatballs*. More recently, "You Don't Own Me" made a ghostly resurrection on the FX channel's sinister, suspenseful series, *American Horror Story*.

In fact, the very presence of Lesley Gore ushered in an era for female soloists and burned a path in the clearing for European imports Dusty Springfield and Petula Clark; stretching beyond epochs, acts like Tiffany, Debbie Gibson, Madonna, Alanis Morissette, Lisa Loeb, Gwen Stefani, Britney Spears, Christina Aguilera, Amy Winehouse, Lily Allen, Katy Perry, Lana Del Rey, and Lady Gaga can all look back at Lesley Gore's footnotes in teen pop history as a pinpoint of influence, a musical butterfly effect. Producer Cevin Soling told this author, "When the whole 'riot grrrl' [a female punk rock crusade in the '90s] and 'girl power' movement was going on, I kept expecting the new wave of feminist rockers to reach out and acknowledge the contributions of the past, but some of them simply acted as if they were the first to make any such statements." Gore was a worthy, early rock suffragette; her palpable force was simply rounded by softer edges. She shined her flashlight up through the floorboards so future generations of girl rockers could see what they were standing upon, and where they were headed.

On Monday, February 16, 2015, worldwide media outlets were stunned when Lois Sasson broke the news that Lesley Gore had died of lung cancer at New York-Presbyterian Hospital in Manhattan. "She was a wonderful human being," Sasson told the Associated Press. "Caring, giving, a great feminist, great woman, great human being, great humanitarian." Following an MRI that revealed a spinal tumor that had been causing the singer back pain, Lesley was given the devastating diagnosis and would live for only one more month. A close friend of Gore's assured this author that her passing was quick and that she did not suffer.

Even longtime fans were stunned by her sudden death and its cause—a testament to the protectiveness with which she shielded her private life. She rarely spoke of Lois to media outlets, managing to shelter their relationship even while the pair made public appearances together at shows and exhibits. In the mid-2000s, when a journalist interviewing Gore following the release of *Ever Since* asked questions pertaining to her religious beliefs and to Lois, the singer skillfully veered the conversation away from those sensitive topics and back to the album; the observant interviewer would later joke in his article about Gore's guardedness. Phil Ramone similarly alluded to Gore's distinct separation of private and professional life, telling this author, "She wasn't a big self-promoter. She didn't need to put her whole personal life out there. She just went out there and did her thing." No one but the closest within her tight inner circle was aware of Gore's illness and her quiet, brief but courageous fight against it.

The shocked and sad response from around the globe was instantaneous. Within hours of the breaking news, fans drove Gore's name to #2 on the Twitter chart that documents trending topics of conversation, and "You Don't Own Me" followed her to the #7 spot. Colleagues of the singer immediately took to the Internet to post their heartfelt tributes. Quincy Jones told *Entertainment Tonight*, "It is important to remember that at one point, the only group that surpassed her in the pop charts was the Beatles. It was a privilege to have been a part of Lesley's life personally and professionally from those early days until now, and although I will miss her deeply, her essence will remain with us always through her music."

Lou Christie began his remembrance to the *Examiner* with the sad opening line, "This is truly the last thing I would want to do, to say good-bye to someone whom I have admired my whole career." He praised her voice and her fierce independence, accolades that were shared in loving acknowledgments from other record-hop idols Brian Wilson, Darlene Love, Neil Sedaka, and Ronnie Spector, whose friendship with Gore spanned fifty-two years.

Even more devastating was that the cancer would attack that which Gore held most dear—her voice, which she cultivated, trained, and perfected over five decades. Blake Morgan, who called Gore his "rock and roll godmother," quipped in an interview on NPR that Lesley was the one who taught him how to drive and how to smoke, though Lois Sasson maintained that her partner was in fact not a smoker, that the singer never gave in to her generation's deadliest vice. In an article by Seattle oncologist H. Jack West, the doctor confirms that a sizable 15 percent of lung cancer patients are actually nonsmokers, owing to several significant health risks like exposure to second-hand smoke and unfavorable, susceptible genetics. His argument, written in response to the pop star's death, seemed to support Sasson's assertion.

Three days after her death, on an icy Thursday morning in New York City, Lesley Gore's memorial was held at the Frank E. Campbell Funeral Home on Madison Avenue. She was laid to rest on February 19, survived by her widow, her brother, and her mother. As Ronny Gore left the funeral home, she was stopped by a gray-haired woman who had been waiting outside. "She said that she had to see me about something," Ronny explained to this author. "She went in after Lesley had passed to disconnect her from some of the equipment, and she heard someone humming. Lesley and the nurse were the only two in the room, and she heard humming." Even in the singer's final moments, Lesley Gore couldn't stop making music.

In his eloquent opinion piece, writer James Rosen grieved, "Her death plunges [us] into a kind of existential loneliness, as in: How can we be living in a time without Lesley Gore and all she represented? Some part of modernity just died!"

Hopefully, the stories, facts, and details presented in this biography effectively support and prove the more focused, explicit claim that forms the bedrock beneath this chronological document and collection of chart numbers—that Lesley Gore deserves the recognition as a pioneer of early American rock and roll, to be restored, and remain, among the rank of habitually celebrated pilgrims as Elvis, Buddy Holly, Connie Francis, Neil Sedaka, and Carole King, for the same reasons they are also justifiably remembered—for her exploration of myriad themes and styles, for experimenting with sound and composition, for contributing to the growth of other artists, for exploring the dangerous territories beyond the safe confines that had been constructed for (and against) her, of ruined birthday parties, mutinous gal pals, and feral boyfriends.

More than fifty years after Lesley performed at her first record hop as an established teenage celebrity, she continued to work, continued to create, continued to wield a tremendous presence. She teased fans that another album was in the works, and she could often be spotted at events that supported the theater and the arts. Up until her death, Gore was at work on a stage play about her early, swift rise to fame, and with her stellar collection of songs fashioning what will be an established soundtrack of recognizable, beloved hits, there should be no problem finding the appreciative, excited audiences that also crowded arenas and playhouses to see the Four Seasons' story in *Jersey Boys*, or the Shirelles' rise to fame portrayed in *Baby It's You*, or the film release of the James Brown story.

In the meantime, we scour the Internet for interviews, anecdotes, fan stories, and photos. Cities lucky enough to have hosted her remember her visits, what stops she made along the classic Route 66 to perform her hits for jukebox revivals and Golden Era rock revues.

In the meantime, we cling to our *Playbill* copies and remember her presence on the stage, recalling her habit of dropping by the wings of smaller theaters downtown to see if she could lend a hand to a younger generation of composers, songwriters, and performers.

In the meantime, we rest the needle on the vinyl and sing along to "It's My Party," belt out the lyrics of "You Don't Own Me," soak in the quiet intensity behind "Ever Since," or get lost along the dusty back roads, dells, and hollows of the rich musical soundscape that basks, glowing, in *Someplace Else Now*.

Her mark on American pop music is eternal, and her first single prophetically guaranteed her legacy for fans and music lovers: "Play all my records, keep dancing all night. . . ."

# Discography

The following discography represents Lesley Gore's releases in the United States, and the peak positions represent the highest that songs and albums reached on *Billboard* music charts.

## Singles

| | | | |
|---|---|---|---|
| Apr 1963 | Mercury 72119 | It's My Party / Danny | (#1) |
| Jun 1963 | Mercury 72143 | Judy's Turn to Cry / Just Let Me Cry | (#5) |
| Sep 1963 | Mercury 72180 | She's a Fool / The Old Crowd | (#5) |
| Dec 1963 | Mercury 72206 | You Don't Own Me / Run, Bobby, Run | (#2) |
| Mar 1964 | Mercury 72259 | That's the Way Boys Are / That's the Way the Ball Bounces | (#12) |
| May 1964 | Mercury 72270 | I Don't Wanna Be a Loser / It's Gotta Be You | (#37) |
| Jul 1964 | Mercury 72309 | Maybe I Know / Wonder Boy | (#14) |
| Oct 1964 | Mercury 72352 | Hey Now / Sometimes I Wish I Were a Boy | (#76) |
| Dec 1964 | Mercury 72372 | Look of Love / Little Girl Go Home | (#27) |
| Mar 1965 | Mercury 72412 | All of My Life / I Cannot Hope for Anyone | (#71) |
| Jun 1965 | Mercury 72433 | Sunshine, Lollipops, and Rainbows / You've Come Back | (#13) |
| Sep 1965 | Mercury 72475 | My Town, My Guy and Me / A Girl in Love | (#32) |
| Nov 1965 | Mercury 72513 | I Won't Love You Anymore (Sorry) / No Matter What You Do | (#80) |
| Jan 1966 | Mercury 72530 | We Know We're in Love / That's What I'll Do | (#78) |
| Mar 1966 | Mercury 72553 | Young Love / I Just Don't Know If I Can | (#50) |
| Jun 1966 | Mercury 72580 | Off and Running / I Don't Care | (#108) |
| Sep 1966 | Mercury 72611 | Treat Me Like a Lady / Maybe Now | (#115) |

| | | | |
|---|---|---|---|
| Jan 1967 | Mercury 72649 | California Nights / I'm Going Out (The Same Way I Came In) | (#16) |
| May 1967 | Mercury 72683 | Summer and Sandy / I'm Fallin' Down | (#65) |
| Sep 1967 | Mercury 72726 | Brink of Disaster / On a Day Like Today | (#82) |
| Nov 1967 | Mercury 72759 | Magic Colors / It's a Happening World [unreleased] | |
| Feb 1968 | Mercury 72787 | Small Talk / Say What You See | (N/A) |
| May 1968 | Mercury 72819 | He Gives Me Love / Brand New Me | (N/A) |
| Aug 1968 | Mercury 72842 | I Can't Make It Without You / Where Can I Go | (N/A) |
| Nov 1968 | Mercury 72867 | I'll Be Standing By / Look the Other Way | (N/A) |
| Feb 1969 | Mercury 72892 | Take Good Care (of My Heart) / I Can't Make It Without You | (N/A) |
| Feb 1969 | Mercury 72892 | Take Good Care (of My Heart) / You Sent Me Silver Bells | (N/A) |
| May 1969 | Mercury 72931 | 98.6 (Lazy Day) / Summer Symphony          (#36, *Easy Listening Chart*) | |
| Sep 1969 | Mercury 72969 | Wedding Bell Blues / One by One | (N/A) |
| Jan 1970 | Crewe 338 | Why Doesn't Love Make Me Happy / Tomorrow's Children | (N/A) |
| May 1970 | Crewe 343 | Come Softly to Me / Billy 'n' Sue's Love Theme (Instrumental) | (N/A) |
| Sep 1970 | Crewe 344 | When Yesterday Was Tomorrow / Why Me, Why You | (N/A) |
| Mar 1971 | Crewe 601 | Back Together / Quiet Love | (N/A) |
| Oct 1972 | MoWest MW5029 | She Said That / Not Me | (N/A) |
| Jun 1975 | A&M 1710 | Immortality / Give It to Me, Sweet Thing | (N/A) |
| Aug 1976 | A&M 1829 | Sometimes / Give It to Me, Sweet Thing          (#8, *Disco Chart*) | |
| May 1986 | Manhattan B50039 | Medley: Since I Don't Have You— It's Only Make Believe / Our Love Was Meant to Be | (NA) |

## Albums

Jun 1963    *I'll Cry If I Want To*      (#24)
Mercury MG20805/SR60805
It's My Party, Cry Me a River, Cry, Just Let Me Cry, Cry and You Cry Alone, No More Tears Left to Cry, Judy's Turn to Cry, I Understand, I Would, Misty, What Kind of Fool Am I, The Party's Over

Nov 1963    *Lesley Gore Sings of Mixed-Up Hearts*      (#51)
Mercury MG20849/SR60849
She's a Fool, The Old Crowd, Fools Rush In, Hello Young Lover, My Foolish Heart, Sunshine, Lollipops, and Rainbows, You Don't Own Me, Run Bobby Run, Young and Foolish, I Struck a Match, If That's the Way You Want It, Time to Go

May 1964    *Boys, Boys, Boys*      (#39)
Mercury MG20901/SR60901
That's the Way Boys Are, It's Gotta Be You, Something Wonderful, You Name It, Danny, I Don't Wanna Be a Loser, That's the Way the Ball Bounces, Leave Me Alone, Don't Call Me (I'll Call You), I'll Make It Up to You, I'm Coolin' No Foolin'

Sep 1964    *Girl Talk*      (#85)
Mercury MG20943/SR60943
Hey Now, Live and Learn, Say Good-bye, Look of Love, You've Come Back, Maybe I Know, Sometimes I Wish I Were a Boy, Little Girl Go Home, I Died Inside, Wonder Boy, Movin' Away, It's Just About That Time

Sep 1965    *My Town, My Guy, and Me*      (#90)
Mercury MG21042/SR61042
My Town, My Guy, and Me, What's a Girl Supposed to Do, What Am I Gonna Do with You, You Didn't Look 'Round, I Don't Care, No Matter What You Do, The Things We Did Last Summer, A Girl in Love, Baby That's Me, Just Another Fool, Let Me Dream, Before and After

Jan 1966    *Lesley Gore Sings All About Love*      (#66)
Mercury MG21066/SR61066
Young Love, I Won't Love You Anymore (Sorry), With Any Other Girl, Too Young, Start the Party Again, That's What I'll Do, Only Last Night, To Know Him Is to Love Him, I Can Tell, We Know

We're in Love, Will You Still Love Me Tomorrow, I Just Can't Get
Enough of You

May 1967    *California Nights*                                      (#69)
Mercury MG21120/SR61120
California Nights, Treat Me Like a Lady, Bad, I'm Going Out
(The Same Way I Came In), Maybe Now, Love Goes on Forever,
Off and Running, Lilacs and Violets, The Bubble Broke, Cry Like
a Baby

[Unreleased]    *Magic Colors* (1967)                         (N/A)
Mercury SR61148
Brink of Disaster, On a Day Like Today, Where Can I Go, You
Sent Me Silver Bells, I'm Fallin' Down, He Won't See the Light,
Magic Colors, How Can I Be Sure, To Sir with Love, It's a
Happening World

Jul 1972    *Someplace Else Now*                              (N/A)
MoWest MW117L
For Me, The Road I Walk, Out of Love, She Said That, Don't
Wanna Be One, Be My Life, Where Do You Go (When You Get
Home), What Did I Do Wrong, Someplace Else Now, Mine, No
Sad Songs, For You

May 1976    *Love Me by Name*                                (N/A)
A&M SP4564
Sometimes, Paranoia, Love Me By Name, Immortality, Can't
Seem to Live Our Good Times Down, Don't Stop Me, Along
the Way, Give It to Me Sweet Thing, Love Me By Name
(Reprise)

Jul 1982    *The Canvas Can Do Miracles*                  (N/A)
51 West Q16261
It's Too Late, Here You Come Again, Haven't Got Time for the
Pain, You're the One That I Want, Daniel, Sailing, To Love
Somebody, Higher and Higher, We're All Alone, Chapel
of Love

May 2005    *Ever Since*                                    (N/A)
Engine Company Records ECR0506014
Ever Since, Cool Web, It's Gone, Someday, Better Angels, You
Don't Own Me, Not the First, Words We Don't Say, Out Here On
My Own, We Went So High

## Notable Collections

Jul 1965     *The Golden Hits of Lesley Gore*            (#65)
Mercury MG21024/R61024
It's My Party, She's a Fool, Judy's Turn to Cry, Just Let Me Cry,
All of My Life, That's the Way Boys Are, You Don't Own Me,
Maybe I Know, Hey Now, Look of Love, I Don't Wanna Be a
Loser, Sunshine, Lollipops, and Rainbows

1987     *The Golden Hits of Lesley Gore*            (N/A)
Mercury 8366882
It's My Party, Judy's Turn to Cry, Just Let Me Cry, She's a Fool,
The Old Crowd, You Don't Own Me, That's the Way Boys Are, I
Don't Wanna Be a Loser, Maybe I Know, Wonder Boy, Hey Now,
Look of Love, Sunshine, Lollipops, and Rainbows, My Town My
Guy and Me, You Didn't Look 'Round, What Am I Gonna Do with
You, Off and Running, California Nights

1994     *It's My Party!*            (N/A)
Germany Bear BCD 15-742-EI

Disc 1
Hello Young Lover, Something Wonderful, It's My Party, Danny,
The Party's Over, Judy's Turn to Cry, Just Let Me Cry, Misty, Cry
Me a River, I Would, No More Tears, Cry and You Cry Alone, I
Understand, Cry, Sunshine, Lollipops, and Rainbows [album
version], What Kind of Fool Am I, If That's the Way You Want It,
She's a Fool, I'll Make It Up to You, The Old Crowd, I Struck a
Match, Consolation Prize, Run Bobby Run, Young and Foolish,
Fools Rush In, My Foolish Heart, That's the Way the Ball
Bounces, After He Takes Me Home [single voice], After He Takes
Me Home [double-tracked voice], You Don't Own Me [mono],
You Don't Own Me [stereo], Time to Go, You Name It

Disc 2
That's the Way Boys Are, Boys, I'm Coolin' No Foolin', Don't Deny
It, I Don't Wanna Be a Loser, It's Gotta Be You, Leave Me Alone,
Don't Call Me (I'll Call You), Look of Love, Wonder Boy, Secret
Love, Maybe I Know, Live and Learn, Sometimes I Wish I Were a
Boy, Hey Now, I Died Inside, Movin' Away, It's Just About That
Time, Little Girl Go Home, Say Good-bye, You've Come Back,
That's the Boy, All of My Life, What's a Girl Supposed to Do,

Before and After, I Cannot Hope for Anyone, I Don't Care, You Didn't Look 'Round

Disc 3

Baby That's Me, No Matter What You Do, Sunshine, Lollipops, and Rainbows [single version], What Am I Gonna Do with You, It's All in the Game, Love Look Away, Let It Be Me, When Sunny Gets Blue, What Am I Gonna Do with You, A Girl in Love, Just Another Fool, My Town My Guy and Me, Let Me Dream, The Things We Did Last Summer, Start the Party Again, I Can Tell, I Won't Love You Anymore (Sorry), I Just Can't Get Enough of You, Only Last Night, Any Other Girl, I Can Tell, To Know Him Is to Love Him, Young Love, Too Young, Will You Love Me Tomorrow, We Know We're in Love, Yeah Yeah Yeah That Boy of Mine, That's What I'll Do, Lilacs and Violets, Off and Running, Happiness Is Just Around the Corner

Disc 4

Hold Me Tight, Cry Like a Baby, Treat Me Like a Lady, Maybe Now, The Bubble Broke, California Nights, I'm Going Out (The Same Way I Came In), Bad, Love Goes On Forever, Summer and Sandy, I'm Fallin' Down, Brink of Disaster, On a Day Like Today, Where Can I Go, You Sent Me Silver Bells, I'm Fallin' Down, He Won't See the Light, Magic Colors, How Can I Be Sure, To Sir with Love, It's a Happening World, Small Talk, Say What You See, He Gives Me Love, Brand New Me, I Can't Make It Without You, Look the Other Way, Take Good Care (Of My Heart), I'll Be Standing By

Disc 5

Ride a Tall White Horse, 98.6 (Lazy Day), Summer Symphony, All Cried Out, One by One, Wedding Bell Blues, Got to Get You Into My Life, Good-bye Tony, Musikant, So Sind Die Boys Alle, Nur Du Allein, Hab Ich Das Verdient, Der Erste Tanz, Little Little Liebling, Sieben Girls, Tu T'En Vas, Je Ne Sais Plus, Je N'ose Pas, Si Ton Coeur Le Desire, Je Sais Qu'Un Jour, C'Est Trop Tard, Eh! Non, Te Voila, Judy's Turn to Cry [Italian], You Don't Own Me [Italian]

## Notable Recordings/Contributions

1966      "Little Sister" / "Things Go Better with Coke" (Coca-Cola radio jingles)

1976 *Taught By Experts* by Peter Allen
A&M Records SP4584
"The More I See You" [background vocals], "She Loves to Hear the Music"

1981 Fame *Original Motion Picture Soundtrack*
PolyGram Records B000001F2B
"Out Here On My Own, Hot Lunch Jam" [both written by Lesley Gore]

1982 *All My Children* Television Show
"Easy to Say, Hard to Do" [written/performed by Lesley Gore]

1983 *It's No Crush, I'm in Love* Television Movie
"My Wildest Dreams" [written/performed by Lesley Gore]

1996 *Music from* The Life
RCA-Victor 09026680012
"My Body"

Grace of My Heart: *Original Motion Picture Soundtrack*
MCA B000002P4S
"My Secret Love" [written by Lesley Gore]

1998 *Grease Is the Word: Boppin' Tunes from the Movie Soundtrack*
Rhino R275275
"Look at Me I'm Sandra Dee," "It's Raining on Prom Night," "Freddy My Love," "There Are Worse Things I Can Do," "We Go Together"[ensemble]

1999 *Sounds for the Soul*
New Jersey Benefit Project SS711
"All One Family" [duet with Michael-Demby Cain]

Superstar: *Dare to Dream—Music from the Motion Picture*
Jellybean Records

"You Wanna Be a Star (Superstar)" [written by Lesley and Michael Gore]

2002 *When Pigs Fly: Songs You Never Thought You'd Hear*
Xemu Records #1010
"Dirty Deeds Done Dirt Cheap"

2004 *Happy Holidays Las Vegas*
Vezzo Records
"Christmas in Las Vegas" [duet with Clint Holmes]

2006      *For the One Who Kills Tomorrow* [Shimmerplanet]
          Shark Meat Records
          "Siren" [featuring Lesley Gore]
2008      *Hallways: The Songs of Carol Hall*
          LML Music #225
          "Hungry for You" [co-written with Carol Hall, performed by
          Lesley Gore]

## Unreleased/Lost Recordings

Mercury Records (1963–1969)
          Baby You Slay Me, Life Is Other People, Make Every Minute
          Count, A New Way to Say I Love You, You've Let Yourself Go,
          Pretend, Teen Years, I Can't Get Him Out of My Mind, When We
          Get There, Sweet as Sugar, Wasn't Loving You Enough, Sixteen
          Candles, I'm in Love Today, The Heart of Town, Lost and Found,
          Sleep Tight, I'm with You, Me About You, Here There and
          Everywhere

Crewe (1970–1971)
          Hey Jude/Cry Me a River (Medley), It Look a Long Time, Does
          Anybody Care About Tomorrow

A&M (1975–1976)
          The Golden Couple, Child, Along the Way [alternate version], I'd
          Like to Be

Midder (1990)
          Together [duet with James Lewis]

# Bibliography

Alden, Oliver. "Love Her by Name: A Lesley Gore Tribute." *www.gullbuy.com*. October 2001.

Allio, Jim. "I'll Cry if I Want To." *www.patswayne.com*. March 1998.

———, "The Great Lost Lesley Gore Album." *www.patswayne.com*. June 2001.

Bashe, Philip. *Teenage Idol, Travelin' Man. The Complete Biography of Rick Nelson*. New York: Hyperion, 1992.

Bessman, Jim. "Lesley Gore: An Appreciation." *Examiner*. February 2015.

Betrock, Alan. *Girl Groups: The Story of a Sound*. New York: Delilah Books, 1982.

Bever, Lindsey. "Lesley Gore: How She Went from 'It's My Party' to 'You Don't Own Me.'" *Washington Post*. February 17, 2015.

*Biography: Lesley Gore*. A&E Home Video, 2001.

Bronson, Fred. Liner notes, *Lesley Gore: The Mercury Anthology*. Polygram, 1996.

Brown, John. "My Town—Lesley Gore: Act One Finale." *YouTube*. Video clip. December 2012.

Burgel, Sheila. Liner notes, *Girl Talk*. Ace Records, March 4, 2014.

Chernikoff, Helen. "Jewish Feminism Chai." *www.thejewishweek.com*. October 2012.

Clemente, John. *Girl Groups: Fabulous Females That Rocked the World*. Wisconsin: Krause Publications, 2000.

Clements, Erin. "Woman Who Inspired 'It's My Party' Reveals Story Behind the Song's Catchphrase." *Today.com*. February 2015.

Crowley, Candy. "Remembering Bobby Kennedy: Thirty Years Later."*www .cnn.com/allpolitics*. June 1998.

Davis, Patricia. "Lesley Gore in Comeback with College Degree." *Pittsburg Press*. June 6, 1969.

Diamond, Morris. *The Name Dropper*. Georgia: Bear Manor Media, 2011.

DiOrio, Al. *Bobby Darin*. Philadelphia: Running Press, 2004.

Dziemianowicz, Joe. "Broadway Pulled Together to Resuscitate New York City After Sept. 11 Attacks." *New York Daily News*. September 7, 2011.

Dolin, Eva. "The Princess . . . of Song." Source unknown, circa 1963, posted at *www.patswayne.com*.

Eckstine, Edward. *Love Me by Name Songbook*, 1976.

Eden, Dawn. Liner notes, *Lesley Gore: It's My Party, the Mercury Discography*. Bear Family Music, 1994.

Evanier, David. *Roman Candle: The Life of Bobby Darin*. Pennsylvania: Rodale, 2004.

Ferrari, Valeria. "Amy's Party: Winehouse Comeback with Lesley Gore Cover This November." *Yahoo News*. September 2010.

Foos, Richard. Liner notes, *Grease Is the Word: Boppin' Tunes from the Hit Movie*. Rhino Records, 1998.

Glitz, Michael. "Singing Her Own Tune." *The Advocate*. January 2006.

Goldstein, Toby. "Review: *Love Me by Name*." *Crawdaddy*. August 1976.

Gore, Lesley. "I Was a New Girl in Town and Felt This Big." Source unknown, circa 1969.

Grimes, William. "Richard Nader, Oldies' Biggest Fan, Dies at 69." *New York Times*. December 2009.

Hendrickson, Tad. "Review: *Happy Holidays Las Vegas*." December 2005.

Hill, Charles G. "Review: *Love Me by Name*." *www.dustbury.com*. 1997.

———, "Review: *Someplace Else Now*." *www.dustbury.com*. 1997.

Interview, Lesley Gore. *www.digitalinterviews.com*. May 2002.

Jewell, Shannon. "Byner, Miss Gore Revive Nostalgia for Dating Days." Source unknown, circa 1973, posted at *www.patswayne.com*.

Jones, Quincy. *Q: The Autobiography of Quincy Jones*. New York: Random House, 2001.

Joyce, Mike. "Lesley Gore: Ever Since." *Washington Post*. September 2005.

Kean, Thomas, et al. "The 9/11 Commission Report." New York: W.W. Norton. 2004.

Lance, Gina. "Icons: Women We Adore: Lesley Gore." *Girl Talk Magazine*. January 2003.

Lanza, Joseph. *Vanilla Pop: Sweet Sounds from Frankie Avalon to ABBA*. Chicago: Chicago Review Press, 2005.

Lefkowitz, David. *www.playbill.com*. August 1997.

"Lesley and Connie Talk About Boys! Boys! Boys!" Unknown source, circa 1963.

"Lesley Gore, 'It's My Party' Songstress Dies at 68." *Entertainment Tonight*. www.etonline.com. February 2015.

"Lesley Gore, Who Sang 'It's My Party' and 'You Don't Own Me,' Died of Lung Cancer." *Althouse*. February 2015.

"Lesley Gore's Partner Reveals New Details About the Singer's Sudden Passing." *Closer Weekly*. February 25, 2015.

Lewis, Barbara. "Singer Leslie [sic] Gore Makes Comeback." *The Lorain Ohio Journal*. July 1972.

Linn, Sarah. "Cambria Resident John Madara Is a Part of Rock 'n' Roll History." *The Tribune (San Luis Obispo)*. February 2014.

Lonergan, Patricia. "It's Their Party: Lesley Gore and Her Music a Hit for YCP." *Spectator*. June 2004.

Lorber, Alan. "The Making of All About Love." *Lesley Gore: It's My Party, The Mercury Discography*. Bear Family Music, 1994.

Mayshark, Jesse Fox. "It's Lesley Gore's Career, She'll Revive It if She Wants To." *New York Times*. October 2005.

McAleer, Dave. *The Book of Hit Singles: Top 20 Charts from 1954 to the Present Day*. New York: Backbeat Books, 2001.

Mills, James. "Lesley Gore: It's Her Party, and She's Bringing It to Palm Springs." *Frontiers Magazine*, posted March 18, 2013.

"No Invitation for Lesley Gore." Source unknown, circa 1964.

Penn, Denise. "It's Still Her Party: An Interview with Sixties Legend Lesley Gore." *Lesbian News*, No. 12, July 2006.

Raab, Lauren. "Lesley Gore, 'It's My Party' and 'You Don't Own Me' Singer, Dies At 68." *New York Times*. February 2015.

Ramone, Phil. *Making Records*. New York, Hyperion: 2007.

Roberts, Jack. "Morris Diamond Profile." *HollywoodHillsGroup.com*. 2013.

Rosen, James. "Opinion: In Tribute to Lesley Gore, Singular Chronicler of Teenage Angst." *NorthJersey.com*. February 2015.

Shewey, Don. "Review: *Love Me by Name*." Boston. 1976.

Staff. "Review: *Love Me by Name*." *Billboard*. May 1976.

———, "Review: *Love Me by Name*." *Creem*. January 1977.

———, "Review: *Love Me by Name*." *Variety*. May 1976.

Swartz, Shauna. "Lesley Gore." *www.afterellen.com*. June 2005.

Waters, John. Liner notes, *Hairspray: Original Motion Picture Soundtrack*. MCA Records, 1988.

West, H. Jack. "How Did Non-Smoker Lesley Gore Get Lung Cancer?" *www.quora.com*. February 2015.

Williams, Richard. *Phil Spector: Out of His Head*. London: Omnibus, 2003.

Young, Harry. Liner notes, *Enlightnin'ment: The Best of Lou Christie*. Rhino Records, 1988.

Zinn, Howard. *A People's History of the United States: 1492–Present*. New York: Harper, 1999.

# Index